A
MONK
IN THE
WORLD

"Teasdale's account of spiritual life in the midst of the city touched me with its compassionate understanding of the real dimensions of the search for God and the moral work of growing our souls. Although he writes from another tradition than mine, he is an ecumenical and post-triumphalist pilgrim. Reading how he shares his rich contemplative life, I felt often the tug of spirit refreshing me in my own devotion. He will most likely do the same for you."

— Rabbi Zalman Schachter-Shalomi,
Naropa University, co-author of *From Age-ing to Sage-ing*

"This book is where the "growing edge" is: available spirituality drawn from the world's great traditions, our path to a viable future. Inter-spirituality for the millions: an eminently readable and applicable guide to a beautiful life."

— Beatrice Bruteau, author of *Radical Optimism* and
What We Can Learn from the East

"This wonderful book helps us learn how to integrate the fundamental principles of contemplative spirituality into our modern lives. In the nonsectarian monk-in-the-world spirit of Thomas Merton and Bede Griffiths, Brother Wayne has opened the mystic heart and noble mind of a monk in order to show us the many sacred opportunities we can find in our own lives for sharing his own contemplative vocation and delighting in the world without being overcome by it."

— Lama Surya Das, author of *Awakening the Buddhist Heart*

"With exquisite sincerity, beauty, and wisdom, Brother Wayne offers an inspiring model of living an authentic life, participating in the bazaar of life with a heart fragrant with love, truth, and spaciousness."

— Jamal Rahman, Sufi teacher and author
of *The Fragrance of Islam*

"*A Monk in the World* will have a wide readership: Many who just can't join a monastery suspect, nonetheless, that they are somehow monks at heart. They will be thrilled by this book, in which a monk-without-a-monastery reveals intimate glimpses of his life and convictions."

— Brother David Steindl-Rast, OSB, www.gratefulness.org

A
MONK
IN THE
WORLD

CULTIVATING A SPIRITUAL LIFE

WAYNE TEASDALE

FOREWORD BY KEN WILBER

NEW WORLD LIBRARY
NOVATO, CALIFORNIA

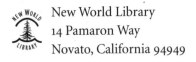
New World Library
14 Pamaron Way
Novato, California 94949

Cover and interior design: Mary Ann Casler

Library of Congress Cataloging-in-Publication Data
Teasdale, Wayne.
  A monk in the world : cultivating a spiritual life / by Wayne Teasdale ; foreword by Ken Wilber.
      p.   cm.
Includes index.
ISBN 1-57731-181-7 (hardcover : alk. paper)
ISBN 1-57731-437-9 (paperback : alk. paper)
1. Spiritual life—Catholic Church. 2. Teasdale, Wayne. I. Title.
BX2350.65 .T44 2002
255—dc21   2002001425

First paperback printing, October 2003
ISBN 1-57731-437-9
Printed in Canada on 100% post-consumer recycled paper
Distributed to the trade by Publishers Group West

10 9 8 7 6 5 4 3 2 1

To Thomas Keating,
my spiritual father, brother, and friend

CONTENTS

ACKNOWLEDGMENTS

There are so many people to whom I owe a debt of gratitude, especially those who have contributed something to my vision of living as a mystic in the world. First, I wish to express my deep appreciation and friendship for my literary agent, Joseph Durepos, and my editor at New World Library, Jason Gardner, both of whom have given so much of their time and energy to shepherding this book into print. Thank you to Jim Somerville and Beatrice Bruteau, especially for her invaluable assistance with the text. I would be remiss if I didn't mention a special circle of friends in Chicago who rallied around me when I had a bout with cancer. In particular, I want to remember Diane Kelleher; Barbara Fields Bernstein; Terry Burson; Josie and Patrick Evans and their children, Shenade, Lauren, Brett, and Zzak; Michael Terrein and Ali, his daughter; Brian Muldoon and his children, Molly, Micky, and Sean; Nick and Carolyn Groves; Bill and Clare Epperly; Nancy Ging; Bill Sheenan; Sean McEntee; Jim Barry; and Judy Walter.

I mention with fondness my friends in the monastic world: Thomas Keating, Theophane Boyd, Basil Pennington, William Mennenger, James Connor, Donald Corcoran, Pascaline Coff, Robert Hale, Bruno Barnhart, Johanna Becker, Katherine Howard, Meg Funk, Gregory Perron, and Terrence Kardong; the Snowmass community; St. Joseph's Abbey in Spencer, Massachusetts, especially Matthew Flynn and Kevin Hunt; the Monastery of Christ in the Desert; Holy Cross Monastery in Chicago; Sacred Heart Monastery in Lisle, Illinois; and New Camaldoli Hermitage in Big Sur, California, and Brother David Steindl-Rast. I would be remiss if I didn't mention my brothers and sisters who are also *sannyasis* here in the states, Brother Francis Ali, Michaela Terrio, Kateri Kautai, Romulad Roberts, and Richard Rosenkranz. Special thanks are expressed to His Holiness the Dalai Lama, his staff in the private office, and especially to Tenzin Choegyal, who is the Ngari Rinpoche, his wife, Rinchen Khando, their children and extended family; to Tenzin Geyche Tethong, Ven. Thakdor, Rinchen Dharlo, Lodi Gyari, Dorjee Wangdue, and the members of the Tibetan community scattered in exile, as well as everyone in the International Campaign for Tibet, including Lesley Fridell, Mary Beth Markey, Bhuchung Tsering, and John Ackerly.

In the Chicago area, I'd like to remember Francis Cardinal George, O.M.I., Lou Cameli, Dan Coughlin, Tom Baima, Joan McGlinchey, Rebecca Armstrong, Andrew Shepherd, Tom O'Bryan, Don Fink, Jennifer Harris, Michael Elliot and all other members of the Friends of Compassion, and the Friends of Bede Griffiths; Felex Machado, Bishop Michael Fitzgerald, and Francis Cardinal Arinze and Chidi Denis Isizoh of the Pontifical Council for Interreligious Dialogue. Then there are all my friends in the Parliament of the World's Religions, especially Bob and Judy Thompson, Jim and Cetta Kenney, Dirk

Ficca, Josh Borkin, Francesca di Britto, Irfan Khan, Rabbi Herb Bronstein and his wife, Tamar, Travis and Gia Rejman, Kevin Coval, and Eboo Patel. There are many others in the Parliament to whom I am grateful, but space does not permit me to list all their names here. I would also like to express thanks to all my friends and associates in Common Ground and at DePaul University, especially Michael Skelley, Nancy Davis, Michael DeAngelis, and Bill Hyashi of Columbia College. At Catholic Theological Union in Chicago, I'd like to mention Don Senior, John Pawlikowski, Mary Frohlich, Scott Alexander, Vaughn Fayle, Barbara Doherty, Horacio Perez, Harietta Holloway, Francise Hawkins, Jim Doyle, Pauline Lerch, Claude Marie Barbour, Joann McCaffrey, Gene Lauer, Robert Ludwig, Ken O'Malley, and all the members of the Passionist Community at C.T.U.

I would like to also acknowledge Bob and Kathy Fastiggi, Francis Tiso, Eric, Sarina, Mila, Yoji, Margie, Michael, Mark, and Hugo Montenegro, Sofina and Glen Rozich, Asa Sandlund and Preston Singletary, Jonathan and Lisanne LaCroix, Robert and Barbara Muller, Steve and Sue Delaronde, Pam Delaney, the Delarondes, Olivia Hobletzelle, Gary Mallalieu, Luke O'Neill Jr., Tommy Sullivan, Martha Howard and Gene Arbetter, Gary and Megan Shunk, Russill and Asha Paul D'Silva, Mohammed Zaffarkhan, David and Naomi Wilkinson, Tim and Barbara Cook, and all the members of the Church of Conscious Harmony in Austin, Texas, and Art DelVesco; Jeff, Lisa, Jordan, Crista, Abby, Hope, Don, Alicia, Greg, Alex, Didi, Max, and Gretchen Genung. Mention should also be made of Gail Fitzpatrick-Hopler, Carl Arico, Ken Warner, Sergio and Chris Rojas, Jamal Rahman, Guy Petruzzelli, Clif and Ibi Matthews, Eric and Sandy Carlson, and Pat Brennen. There are also Jim and Patti Slama; Paula Hardin; Magdalena Gomez and James

Lescault; Simon and Teresa Irizarry; everyone at Sounds True, especially Sarah Wheeler and Matt Lacata.

I would like to thank in a special way Ken Wilber for his visionary foreword, and the many members of the Integral Institute; the faculty, staff, and students of the Institute for Spiritual Leadership; all my students wherever they are; T. J. and Kris McGovern, Larry Korass, Robert Hopper, B. C. and Stacey Calma, Don and Johann Wrona, Darrell and Jeannie Jordan, Bob and Jane McGuffey, Hal and Betsy Edwards, Astarius An, Joel and Gwen Beversluis, the Gustafson family, Rick and Lynn Doblin, Ron Miller, Dan, Trish, Rory, Marshal, Ryan, Kattie and Stockton McEntee, James Klassen, Brennan Young, Matt Paterson, Nathan Katz, Martin Wall, Quincy Fernandez, and Steve Wiseman, Arlo and Jackie Guthrie, Ewert and Janet Cousins, Jeff Jaeger, Lorene Wu and Francis D'Ario, Alan Race, Marcus Braybrooke, and Brent Hunter. And finally, all the members of the Spiritual Life Circle of the Parliament of the World's Religions, especially Harold Kasimow, Omie Baldwin, Asayo Horibe, Joyce Kemp, Kathy and Tory Sarator, Ann Patterson, and Carol Henning.

FOREWORD

This is a beautiful, wonderful, wise book that gently touches and compassionately evokes the deep spirituality in all of us. But more than that, it further invites us — challenges us — to carry that awakened spirituality into the world, thus integrating inner life with outer life, drenching both in a radiance from the realized heart that allows grace the room to do its divine work. A more balanced, a more complete, a more "integral" spirituality — uniting both inner and outer — is the theme of this moving book.

It seems that humankind's spiritual aspirations have often fallen into two major camps, what we might call "this-worldly" and "otherworldly," or earth-oriented and heaven-oriented. The latter portrays salvation as existing in a dimension or realm that is somehow apart from this world, not of this earth, profoundly beyond this plane of existence. Whether this is a mythical heaven beyond earth, or a nirvana divorced from *samsara*, or a contemplative ascent that leaves the senses far behind, we find in these traditions a concerted proclamation that this world is, at best, a prep school for the Divine, and, at worst, an active source of evil, sin, duality, and despair, the escape from which is a prerequisite for salvation.

This-worldly traditions, on the other hand, are headed in more or less the opposite direction. All true liberation and salvation must be found on this earth, in this body, in this life; any aspirations for a transcendental heaven are not only based on childhood illusions, but actively deny and repress present human potentials that alone can lead to a bettering of life for millions of human beings. This-worldly traditions include a wide variety of approaches — from classic paganism to modern Marxism to scientific materialism to virtually all ecology movements — but what they all have in common is the belief that transcendental religions are not only the opiate of the masses, they devastate effective action in the only arena that actually matters — this earth, this world, right here and now.

Is my ultimate salvation to be found in this world or out of it? It seems that the first step to a more integral or comprehensive approach to spirituality would be discovering a way to truly bring together the important truths of both this-worldly compassion and otherworldly realization, thus uniting the immanent and transcendent aspects of a spirituality that charitably embraces both.

But that challenge, daunting enough in itself, is only the first in a series of difficult but incredibly exciting opportunities for discovering a spirituality that is at home in both this world and the other: a heaven that transcends and includes the earth and all its blessed inhabitants, a spirituality that does not cloister its realization but ecstatically shares it with the world, a nirvana not divorced from *samsara* but embracing *samsara* in the radiance of its own self-realization.

It appears that a truly integral spirituality — the spirituality of a monk in the world, of a contemplative heaven embracing this earth — would have to integrate or include a vast range of truths from across the entire spectrum of human possibilities, including not only this-worldly and otherworldly spirituality, but also the undeniable truths of modern science. In short, a truly catholic spirituality, as a matrix of manifestation, would have to include the very best of premodern, modern, and postmodern truths, bound together by a Spirit that transcends all and includes all, that goes beyond but intimately embraces this and all possible worlds.

A tall order, yes? But what is so exhilarating about this quest is that many spiritual adepts and practitioners from around the world are rapidly converging on the outlines of what a truly integral spirituality might look like. This truly catholic spirituality does not deny the revealed truths of any tradition, but gently sets them in the context of each other's realizations, fostering an interspirituality that deepens, not denies, the truths of each. I have suggested one such approach in *A Brief History of Everything*, but the important point is that these approaches are beginning rapidly to emerge around the world, and Brother Wayne, in the following pages, will introduce you to some of the truly great pioneers in this move toward a more integral spirituality — toward a more catholic communion of all souls in the radiance of being, the radiance of a timeless otherworldly Spirit that finds its own body and its own substance and its own realization in the glories of this world, in the pulsing of this earth, in the beating of the hearts of all sentient beings, moved by grace and found by a glory that reminds us all that the temporal and historical are simply the ecstatic self-expressions of the timeless and eternal.

Brother Wayne dedicates this book to Father Thomas

Keating, whom he calls "my spiritual father, brother, and friend," and who, I deeply concur, will be judged by history to be one of the great founding saints of a more integral and catholic spirituality. Brother Wayne discusses several others who, I also agree, are among the founding souls of this more charitable embrace — Thomas Merton, Abhishiktananda, the Dalai Lama, Bede Griffiths, Raimon Panikkar, Brother David Steindl-Rast, Amma, Thich Nhat Hanh, and Rabbi Zalman Schachter (and he certainly would not exclude the great historical forerunners of such, from Plotinus to Lady Tsogyal to the remarkable Sri Aurobindo).

While the timeless truths of Spirit are surely just that — namely, timeless — it appears that the temporal truths of Spirit ceaselessly unfold, with new truths emerging daily, new revelations constantly accumulating, screaming surprises jumping out at us from every corner of Spirit's astonishing creativity, as evolution itself searches secretly through the stream of time that is Spirit's great unfolding sport and play. And it does appear, or so it seems to this poor soul, that today's world — today's modern and postmodern world — is slowly groping its way, guided by the cunning of grace, to find forms of spirituality more intimately suited to the times, which is to say, suited to Spirit's unfolding in this historical arc of its own manifestation.

And it does likewise appear that truly catholic souls such as Brother Wayne will join the ranks of those who are compassionately acting as Spirit's contemplative witness to a yet more encompassing, more compassionate, more glorious embrace, so that each and every sentient being may truly become a monk in this world.

— Ken Wilber
Spring, 2002

Living as a Monk
in the World

It has been said that sometimes we have to go halfway across the world to discover what lies right under our noses. And sometimes what we discover, and the consequences these discoveries generate, become a defining moment for us. My defining moment came in India; what I experienced there has become the foundation of my identity. In 1986, I accepted an invitation to visit Father Bede Griffiths, an English Benedictine monk who had been living in India and studying Hinduism for many years. He invited me to stay with him for a time at Shantivanam, or "Peaceful Grove," a Christian ashram established in 1950 by two Frenchmen, Jules Monchanin and Henri Le Saux, who later became known as Abhishiktananda. Father Bede, who took over the ashram in 1968, was invited to India by a friend to establish a Benedictine monastery on the subcontinent. In 1968 he was asked to assume leadership of Shantivanam when Abishiktananda left to meditate in a cave in the north of India.

Shantivanam is in the village of Tannirpalli, in the southern state of Tamil Nadu, some 280 miles southwest of Madras. It sits on fifty acres on the banks of the Kāveri, one of India's seven sacred rivers, often called the "Ganges of the south." For millennia the land around Shantivanam has been held as sacred, a consecrated place for sages, *sannyasis,* or monks, and mystics. More recently it has become a refuge and sanctuary for countless pilgrims of many different traditions. It is a tiny patch of paradise in the midst of India's poverty, disease, and overpopulation, serious problems of a struggling democracy. Rich in mangos and rice, Shantivanam possesses a beauty, serenity, and peace that welcome the many weary pilgrims who come to it for sanctuary. Once travelers find it, they quickly fall under its spell and don't want to leave.

Into this secluded forest I arrived in early November 1986, already a lay monk from Hundred Acres Monastery, a small religious community in New Hampshire. I first stayed for six months. I then returned for another six months each of the following two years. On my third visit, with the new year approaching, Father Bede sent for me and asked if I would consider taking *sannyasa,* or Indian monkhood, from him as a Christian, not as a Hindu. I hadn't considered this step when I planned this third trip, but to my utter surprise I found myself agreeing before I even had a chance to think about it. I felt a strange peace about his invitation and my decision, even though I wasn't sure I was ready to take such a momentous step.

Several days later, twenty-five of us assembled on the banks of the river an hour before dawn to share in the *sannyasa diksha,* the ceremony of initiation that goes back to the Vedas and the Upanishads, the sacred Hindu texts. We sat in meditation under a grove of eucalyptus trees as we prepared. The river was quiet and still, but nature was awake with life, and across the

Kāveri an eerie chanting emanated from a Hindu temple, a timeless harbinger of the coming day. Although it was cloudy that early morning, an energy moved through the air. The atmosphere seemed charged with countless presences, angelic beings who had come to witness what was about to happen. In India, a *diksha* is a timeless event woven into the fabric of the country's religious history and culture, a sacred occurrence in a spiritual society.

The gentle and sagely Father Bede signaled to a young monk who led us in the *Gayatri* mantra, the most sacred chant of the Indian tradition, found in the Rig Veda, one of the most ancient in the tradition. This was followed by more chants, and then readings from the Upanishads, the Psalms, the Bhagavad Gita, and the Gospel of John. Bede then gave a beautiful discourse on the meaning of *sannyasa,* the ancient roots of renunciation in the life of the *rishis,* the saints, sages, and mystics of Indian antiquity. He described the place of the renunciate in India and in the Church, how the *sannyasi* is a living sign of the transcendent nature of life, of the mystical quest for God, or in Indian terms, the quest for the Absolute.

Father Bede and I approached the edge of the sacred Kāveri. I entered the water and took off my clothes, flinging them into the surface stream, then submerging myself under the water three times. As sunrise quickly approached, and I emerged from the river, Father Bede wrapped me in the *kavi,* the ancient religious garb of the renunciate, the *sannyasi.* This rite of initiation is thousands of years old, and it symbolizes renunciation of the world, of possessions, and of oneself. Quickly I dried myself off, hidden by the morning's pale radiance. Grinning broadly, Father Bede draped me with the *kavi.* Traditionally, the *kavi* consists of two pieces of cloth the color of saffron; one piece is a *dhoti,* worn around the waist and reaching the feet, while the other is worn around the shoulders as a shawl. The garment itself is simple and elegant, part of the national dress of India that men, women, and children all wear. My *kavi* was saffron, the color of purity, representing the *sannyasi*'s goal of freedom from desire.

The *diksha* was a very powerful experience for me. It left an indelible mark on my spiritual life and became a prominent feature in my interior geography. After I took this radical step of *sannyasa,* the life of renunciation, I thought to myself, "Perhaps I should make a home here and stay in India, living right here at Shantivanam." I had fallen under the spell of Shantivanam and the new life that lay before me.

But it was not to be. Hours later, as I sat with Bede on the porch of his hut, he turned to me and with gentle authority said, "Your mission is in the West." I replied that I was thinking I might like to stay at Shantivanam. But he insisted that I return home. "You're needed in America, not here in India." He went on to describe how the *sannyasi*'s life might look in America or Europe. "The real challenge for you, Wayne, is to be *a monk in the world,* a *sannyasi* who lives in the midst of society, at the very heart of things." Although this charge seemed difficult, I accepted it, only later perceiving the wisdom in it. A *sannyasi* always receives a new name, and so Father Bede gave me the Sanskrit name Paramatmananda, which means "bliss of the supreme spirit" or "joy of the holy spirit." I strove to make the name fit me, finding joy and humor in life and sharing them with others.

FROM WITHDRAWAL TO ENGAGEMENT

The way of a *sannyasi* or a *sannyasini* (nun) in India is an acosmic path — that is, not of this world. It transcends the values, attachments, and obligations of worldly existence. As in their

Christian and Buddhist counterparts, the way of the *sannyasi* and *sannyasinin* is a path of withdrawal, a radical extraction from the ways of selfish, purely individualistic pursuits. This withdrawal makes possible a focus on the eternal, changeless reality of the ultimate. The way of the *sannyasi* concentrates one's life and energy on this eternal quest and the difficult work of transformation, a lonely, often desolating activity. The most dramatic and ancient characterization of the acosmic ascetic, the *muni,* or silent seer, is found in the Rig Veda, where this seer is said to be "girded with the wind."[1] This description emphasizes just how unrelated to this world the renunciate is, underscoring the total freedom and detachment of the other-worldly ascetic. The renunciate's commitment is absolute and final, like that of the Buddha two thousand years later or of Christians Francis of Assisi in the thirteenth century and Benedict of Nursia in the fifth. This otherworldly orientation is found throughout the Christian monastic and contemplative tradition and serves as the basis of the Carmelite Order and the influential teachings of the Spanish mystics of the sixteenth century, Teresa of Avila and John of the Cross, as also of the English mystic Julian of Norwich. For the less contemplative, more active orders of the Church, a way of formulating this calling is *in* the world, but not *of* the world.

Without doubt, there is great value in spirituality that emphasizes and supports withdrawal from society. But in our time, with its special needs, we require a spirituality of intense involvement and radical engagement with the world. It is in the real world that people live their busy lives, and it is in the real world that the wisdom of the monks must be made accessible. It is in the real world that their awakening and development need to occur, not off in remote solitude.

The type of engagement I have in mind is direct, not

abstract. It is a twofold engagement: personal encounter with others and a participation in the experiences, struggles, trials, joys, triumphs, and fears most people in society experience. The daily tasks of earning a living, paying bills, saving money, getting along with others, being entertained, enjoying healthy recreation, and learning how to interact with difficult people are all part of an active life. So they must also be part of life for a monk in the world, at the crossroads of contemporary culture and experience. When I use the term *monk in the world* I am referring both to my own situation as a monastic type living in the heart of society and to *you*, who are or aspire to be a contemplative resident in the same busy world. The traditional monastic understanding that one can be *in* the world, but not *of* it can be reformulated as *engaged* in the world, but *free* of it, engaged in the world and with others, but not attached to the world's greed, indifference, insensitivity, noise, confusion, pettiness, unease, tension, and irreverence.

Declaring oneself a monk, or mystic, in the world is a way to make the journey easier. By committing to a way of life, or even simply to a name on which we can hang our attention, we formalize our commitment to treating our actions in the world as important. Many organized religions have realized the necessity of creating institutional positions for those following the practice of their faith. Although we may not all want the structure and tradition of an established path, the formal dedication to becoming a mystic in the world — even if we keep the identification to ourselves — can help us immeasurably as we battle with the endless distractions the world serves up to us. Whether this commitment involves taking the lay monk's full vows of celibacy and the formal practice, as I have done, or simply following a path of spiritual practice and right behavior, a formal commitment, one we can return to in our moments of doubt and distraction, makes a mature spiritual life possible.

THE MONASTERY WITHIN

Monks and nuns live set apart in a consecrated place. Their monastery exists for three reasons: to provide a supportive environment to seek God in a spirit of daily surrender; to provide an ongoing opportunity for genuine Christian — or Buddhist, Hindu, or Jain — love in the practice of acceptance of one another, a place to pursue compassion and selfless love toward each other; and to provide a refuge for people living active lives, those caught up in the distractions of this noisy, confusing, and disordered world. In this last sense, it is a sanctuary for *all* who arrive at the monastery's gate, a place of peace and calm, where the ways of the world do not follow.

The visitors who stay for a time in the monastic retreat or guesthouse come for many reasons. Some are in search of God and of themselves in God. Perhaps they want the simplicity and focus of the monastery, the sane and balanced rhythm of prayer, work, and study. Perhaps they desire the integrated life of a single place rather than the fragmented existence of contemporary life. It may be the sacred values and practices of monasticism or the emphasis on the sacredness of life, nature, cosmos, and one another that draws them. Often it is the deep seriousness and commitment to faith and to transcendent reality that calls them for a brief time to come apart and be renewed in spirit by drinking from the living waters of divine wisdom. Sometimes it is to experience a sacred, timeless culture, one that is less mired in the compulsiveness and insensitivity of modern society. Whatever the reason, for the vast majority who come to these peaceful oases, it is for a very brief time — a weekend, a few days, or a week.

For these seekers, the question becomes how to integrate their glimpse of monastic peace into their everyday lives in the world, how to cultivate contemplation within an active life. To achieve this integration requires the realization that the real monastery exists within them as a dimension of their own consciousness. The important work for all of us in the world is the inner struggle and refinement that goes on in the midst of our daily activities. How do we succeed in dwelling in the cave of our own hearts, in that monastery within? How do we nurture and nourish, inspire and inform, the inner monk that all of us have, and *are,* as an expression of the mystic in us? That is the focus and concern of this book.

THE OUTER AND INNER MONK

Although custom and usage has identified it with male monastics exclusively, the word *monk* is actually a generic term, referring to both male and female monastics. Jean Leclercq (1911–1993), the French Benedictine monastic, theologian, and historian, used to remark that we need a new word that unites the words for monk and nun. With tongue in cheek, he brought the two together and proposed *nunk.* The word *nun* actually refers to female monastics, though it is extended in ordinary usage to any woman religious in vows. Usually a nun is a religious sister who lives under a monastic rule in an enclosed environment, a cloister.

A monk, then, is a person who has dedicated his or her life to seeking God. St. Benedict, in his *Rule,* elevates this activity to the highest level of motivation and proclaims it the definitive criterion for accepting a candidate into the monastery. Brother David Steindl-Rast, an Austrian-born Benedictine monk and one of the leaders of the American interfaith encounter of the last thirty years, once remarked: "If the first thing you think of in the morning when you wake up is God, then you are a monk!" The outer monk, that is, the monk in the regular sense, belongs to a monastery under a rule of life and an abbot, or superior. This monk wears the habit, or religious garb, and takes vows. Being an outer monk, following the traditional monastic community life, often makes possible the inner monk, the mystic within.

Monasticism in all its forms — Eastern, Western, primitive, inventive, contemplative, active, and mixed — exists to nurture the development, fruition, and gifts of the inner mystic or inner monk. We all have this hidden mystic consciousness that desires to be born, grow, and give itself out freely. The contemplative journeys to this goal on which he or she has his heart and mind concentrated in all effort. The contemplative seeks intimacy with the Spirit, with infinite consciousness, vast realization — with God, the hidden divine mystery. The word *mystic* refers to this desire and pursuit of intimacy with the Divine, with the Spirit for the sake of others and for oneself.

Contemplation is essentially the process of acquiring this intimacy, and monasteries are places of cultivating this capacity and gift: *capacity* meaning our own effort and *gift* meaning God's infusion of grace into our inner being. Contemplation is the ultimate purpose of monastic communities. They are environments of intense and comprehensive growth in this most precious of activities. "The essence of monastic life is not its structures but its interior practice, and the heart of interior practice is contemplative prayer," wrote Thomas Keating, the Trappist spiritual teacher.[2] The monk is immersed in contemplative experience, and this is why he or she chooses such a unique way of life. The monastery is not an end in itself, or that place where everything comes together for us, but a means to cultivate the mystic in us, the contemplative vision and gift.

Each person has this gift, or at least access to it, simply by being born. Our birth is an invitation to our gifts, a call to immersion in the Absolute, with the possibility of our ultimate transformation through contact with the Divine. All monastic life must be inspired by this deep desire. Monasticism has its origin here in the hidden places of the heart. Brother David Steindl-Rast expresses it simply: "Monasticism of the heart is the heart of monasticism."[3] It is this *heartfelt* monasticism that has inspired so many souls to venture to mountain caves, desert huts, and remote communities throughout the East and West, whether these seekers be Hindu, Jain, Buddhist, or Christian.

It is the longing of the monk within that calls so many to leave the world for brief retreats. The same call works within both the outer and the inner monk. The outer monk joins the monastery to release the inner monk's mystical life. A monastic is ideally someone who takes the inner monk seriously, and this inner monk is simply the mystic in all of us. Eventually the outer and inner monk become one through prayer, spiritual practice, meditation, or mystical contemplation. All these practices are related to the birth of awareness and to inner attention to the sacred. The monk in all of us, as cross-cultural thinker Raimon Panikkar observes, "aspires to reach the ultimate goal of life with all his [or her] being by renouncing all that is not necessary to it, i.e., by concentrating on this one single and unique goal."[4] Panikkar speaks of the inner monk as essential to the human, as part of each person. Having an inner monk doesn't require an overtly religious context. It is an innate expression of the mystical quest that everyone can reach by virtue of our common humanity. "The monastic vocation as such precedes the fact of being Christian, or Buddhist, or secular, or Hindu, or even atheist," writes Panikkar.[5]

WHY BE A MONK IN THE WORLD?

Is it possible for the masses of humanity, who do not live in monastic seclusion, to activate the monk within? Are we capable of realizing the mystical life here in the world, in the midst of so much frantic activity? That question is the basic preoccupation of this book. Why be a monk in the world and not in a comfortable monastery? For many years I assumed I would find God sequestered away, and surely one can, but I learned a valuable lesson from my time in India. India taught me the primacy of the mystical quest, the search for the Divine Presence by the wandering ascetic renunciate. India incorporated this vital dimension of spiritual life early on in its history. It required that the contemplative life, the monk within, be appointed to the last stage in life — but for everyone, not just for a select few. This was, and remains, the ideal. Although monasteries and other such institutions are useful, they are not necessary for one to make his or her way into this mystery. Once the inner monk awakens, once the mystic begins to see, an interior freedom is ignited, and the external structures become less important. We will always need them, but they are not where humanity lives. They are places of retreat, renewal, and rest. And most important, they are a countercultural symbol of the spiritual journey we must all make in our own way and at our own pace.

Why do I choose to be a monk in the world and not locked away in a remote hermitage? Because I want to identify with and be identified with all those who suffer alone in the world, who are abandoned, homeless, unwanted, unknown, and unloved. I want to know the insecurity and vulnerability they experience, to forge a solidarity with them. The homeless are often open to the divine mystery through their very vulnerability and anxiety. It is also my desire to be close to you, dear reader, especially if you are struggling. At the same time, while embracing this larger world, I identify with all my brothers and sisters in monasteries, hermitages, and retreat centers everywhere and in every tradition.

The Spirit has called me into the world to live a spirituality of engagement with those who suffer, and that's all of us. This call includes kinship with other species and with nature as a whole within this vast cosmos, which is our real community and certainly the context of our life on this fragile planet. I want to be in the bosom of God in the heart of the world. St. Francis of Assisi taught me when I was a child the importance of simplicity of life, what the Catholic tradition calls poverty. The economic pressures of modern life have caused most religious orders to lose sight of the true meaning of simplicity. With the exception of Mother Teresa's Missionaries of Charity and the Little Brothers of Jesus, few orders are able to maintain this ideal. Living as a hermit monk in the world, as a contemplative mystic working for a living, like most people, living simply and consciously, I can do the most good for others.

Furthermore, I choose to be a monk living in the midst of the real world, among my brothers and sisters, because I am first of all a contemplative mystic. That is, I am anchored in a deep and growing inner awareness of God's presence, of the Divine's incomparable love for each one of us. Often I feel the Divine One giving itself to me directly, in my relationships with others and in the natural world; it is always a source of inspiration, delight, and even bliss. I experience and so am aware of this Presence in some way, all the time. Often I am overwhelmed by God's love and I feel it inviting me to profound and subtler degrees of surrender, that is, of greater generosity in assenting to God's invitation. My mystical experience is emphatically and inevitably God centered.

The primary element in my understanding and practice of spiritual life is the inner reality of the Gospel: love itself. The Gospel calls us to intimacy with the Divine and availability to others; these are really two dimensions of the same reality. For me, in my experience of being a Christian in these difficult, uncertain, and confusing times, the Gospel has become self-evident in its eternal truth as an ethics of love. I cannot doubt its reality and truth. As an ethics of love, the Gospel contains, I believe, the principle of life itself. This love, which is Divine Love, incarnated in Christ and in us, is referred to as *agape*, selfless or sacrificial love, pointing to and emphasizing its essential characteristic of unconditional giving. To me, this represents the message of Jesus — an intensely powerful insight on and invitation to being in the world. I am convinced that the Gospel represents a high point in humankind's spiritual, moral, and psychological evolution. The example of Jesus repeatedly comes to me in the course of each day. His message to love selflessly is the substance of my world, the radiating light and truth of how I attempt to dwell in this society on this tiny planet we call our home. I am painfully aware, though, of how often I fail.

My desire to be a monk in the world, rather than in a monastery, has much to do with this compelling and challenging teaching of the Gospel. I wish to be near the least, the forgotten and ignored, so I can be a sign of hope and love for them and for all others who need me in some way. It's here I find my anchor in God's love.

> Come you blessed of my Father, and possess the kingdom prepared for you from the beginning because when I was hungry, you gave me something to eat; when I was thirsty, you gave me something to drink. When I was a stranger, you welcomed me. Naked, and you clothed me;

sick, and you visited me. I was in prison, and you came to me.... Then the just will answer him, saying: Lord, when did we see you hungry, and feed you; thirsty, and give you drink? And when did we see you as a stranger, and welcome you in, or naked, and clothed you? Or when did we see you sick or in prison, and come to you? And the king, answering them, shall say: as often as you did it to the least of my brethren, you did it to me.[6]

These words from the Gospel of Matthew form the hub of my life as a contemplative monk in the world. The world is the rim, while all that I do in relation to my spiritual life and the various activities I pursue, the experiences I share with all those who also live in this same world, constitute the spokes of the wheel of well-being. I now live and work in Chicago. I find the thriving city an exciting place to meet God and to be a monk in the world. Charlie Rich, a monk who lived in Manhattan, once wrote: "The city is a good place for the monk because no one pays attention to him there!"

I hope to illustrate in *A Monk in the World* how one can be a mystic or monk in the world without departing it. This book seeks to inculcate the best of the monastic vision by detailing a number of living elements of a spiritual life in the context of pluralism, interfaith encounter, and contemplative experience but also through a creative spirituality of engagement. This book is not about me, but it does draw on my experience to provide examples of how to live as a monk, or mystic, in the world.

In chapter 1 I reflect on the meaning of the world and how we experience it, on making sense of what we experience in our daily lives. The second chapter deals with divine intimacy, prayer, or spiritual practice — realization and mystical experience. Chapter 3 considers the Church and a new vision of its role in an interspiritual global culture, while chapter 4 explores the nature of friendship and its important role in the spiritual journey. Chapter 5 considers the true value of time, work, and money. The sixth chapter concentrates on the vast problem of the homeless and the role we play as mystics, while the seventh chapter focuses on the struggle for justice and peaceful change. Chapter 8 examines the mystery of suffering and illness and their function in our spiritual growth. Chapter 9 reflects on the phenomenon of interspirituality, of bringing together faith communities worldwide, and chapter 10 examines the true nature of awareness and its importance in the life of a mystic in the world.

Finally, I hope the epilogue will bring these elements together to inspire our collective intention. In using this book in your own spiritual life, I suggest you read it slowly and meditatively, allowing it to speak to the monk or mystic within you. Allow these pages to become a rich soil for cultivating your own kind of engaged spirituality. If enough of us live this way, it could ignite a revolution. The real revolution to come is the spiritual awakening of humankind, and out of that awakening will be born a civilization of love, a universal society with an engaged heart.

CHAPTER 1

The World As Presence and Community

We can never escape the world, no matter how much we try. Yet that is precisely what our human nature urges us to do sometimes. When I first lived in a monastery, I learned very quickly that monastic life did not afford more escape from the world than any other place. Rather, it presented a deeper encounter with it. The monastic life is not a rejection of the world; it is a decision to engage with this world from a different dimension, from the enlarged perspective of love, as perceived by the Gospel in its utter simplicity and clarity.

In a very real sense, we are all integrally part of the world, even if we live in the relative peace of the cloister. I say "relative" because sometimes monasteries are anything but peaceful. They can be islands of turmoil, discontent, and unhappiness. It all depends on where individual members are in their development. If monks or nuns feel ambiguous about their vocation, their spiritual life will be clouded by their doubts, and their monastic experience will reflect a divided heart. If, however, they are confident in their monastic commitment, at peace within, and enjoying a vital spiritual life in union with God, they will be centered deeply in their source of hope. This experience is magnified for a monk, or mystic, in the world.

For me the world has always been an exciting, fearful, and often overwhelming place. The sounds, sights, and frenetic pace of our cities, with their fascinating diversity and physical presence, while compelling, have also challenged me. The world, where anonymity is reinforced by the indifference of strangers and a mass culture that fears intimacy, is fraught with many dangers. Most of us experience this, even if we don't acknowledge it. Even if we feel physically safe, and many do not, we experience so much stimulation from so many directions that it is easy to feel overwhelmed.

As I said in the introduction, to be in the world as a monk, as someone consecrated to God, is first of all to be *in* the world, but not *of* it. This distinction contributes to my unease at times, yet I know I'm not alone in these feelings. For many years as a hermit in the city — and for years before — I really felt like a stranger in a world I didn't understand. It has not always been easy to be a monk living in the heart of a secular culture unsupportive of the spiritual quest. In India and other societies of Asia where there is a larger cultural support system, this is not as much of a problem. But the West is a different kind of place.

The world is, in a sense, a place of exile. We are never fully at home here, and in my tradition, we are taught by St. Paul that we really "don't have a lasting city here."[1] As the Buddha taught in his first noble truth, life is suffering, or as Buddhist psychologist Mark Epstein more accurately translates it, life has "pervasive unsatisfactoriness."[2] We are transients, pilgrims on our way, passing through this vale of tears, snatching a bit of joy where we can from the mouth of death before it devours our dreams. I think the unease people experience, our existential anxiety in the face of this fleeting drama, has much to do with the sense of alienation we feel once we realize our mortality. I have often felt like Jonah in the belly of the great whale, only the whale is not so benign! But whatever my feelings at facing my mortality, I continually look to the sacred in the world, which is so often represented in the realms of nature as well as in the human community.

THE COMMUNITY OF NATURE

More fundamental than the human community, which we so often think of as the "world," is the pervasive presence of nature — a nurturing, omnipresent, and sometimes menacing reality that sustains us in every sense and without which we cannot survive. Nature's surrounding, enveloping presence has always been magical for me, especially as I was growing up in Connecticut. I loved its wildness, its capacity for unbounded freedom. I loved the fragrance of flowers, with their ability to awaken moods, stir distant associations long forgotten, and carry me to magical realms in my imagination. This experience was common during my childhood and acted as a frame of reference in those idyllic years.

Nature has always been a friend, a mysterious presence, a constant source of inspiration, insight, and joy. As a child I never regarded it as an inert material substance, but a living, vibrant reality imposing itself on my life. It captured my imagination. I first became aware of the Divine as the magical in nature, and later as the Presence in everything. The natural world emanates or expresses the mystery of the One beyond all the multiplicity of forms we perceive. This One can be felt moving in all things; its energy pervades everything that is manifested. Nature celebrates it in an endless diversity, an immanent presence ever giving life to everything.

The diaphanous quality and power of the natural world, the realm of wilderness, or wildness, often breaks through our ordinary awareness, our mundane preoccupations, in moments of natural revelation in which something more real and ultimate discloses itself to us when we are receptive. These moments in my life have often been fleeting, but their intensity has changed how I view the Divine and the world as a whole.

On one of my long stays in India, while I was visiting Madras, I was walking in a small pasture near an ocean inlet where some cows were grazing. It was an average winter day, very much like a perfect summer's day in New England. An incredible peace pervaded the field and as I stood there I was enveloped in an intense mystical experience. Butterflies, swallows, and dragonflies were buzzing about serenely, while cows and water buffalos stood munching away at the flowing grass. Other water buffalos were blissfully resting in the coolness of a water hole. The essential timelessness of this scene made me feel I was in the presence of an eternal mystery. The entire experience seemed like a kind of cosmic liturgy to me, much like what Bede Griffiths describes occurring to him when he was a teenager in England.[3] A subtle, mysterious presence, though hidden, was everywhere.

Many years later, in Sri Lanka, at the mountain sanctuary of Sri Pada, or Adam's Peak, the power of the natural world again took hold of my inner life. Although little known in Europe or America, Sri Pada is well known in India and Sri Lanka as a pilgrimage site sacred to four religions: Hinduism, Buddhism, Christianity, and Islam. Pilgrims arrive at Sri Pada at evening to climb the mountain meditatively during the night, reaching the summit at dawn. I arrived there with two friends on a February evening to a steady drizzle. It was already dark, and a thick mist had settled in, enveloping the holy mountain. All the way up the path were soft electric lights, adding to the air of mystery. Every few minutes an eerie bell would toll, inviting weary pilgrims to the summit. Never one to enjoy losing a night's sleep, I wasn't looking forward to the nocturnal ascent, but my two companions were eager to start.

As we began the ascent, I was tired and a little cranky, complaining to myself how I really wanted to be in bed. In truth, I was being a bit of a wimp about it all. As I trudged along in self-pity, two elderly women carrying infants on their backs scurried past me up the steep trail. I felt a little ashamed and resolved to cease my internal whining. As I settled into the six-hour trek — broken only by occasional stops at tea stalls — I found myself reflecting on the meaning of Sri Pada and the pilgrimage I was engaged in. I began to recognize it as a metaphor for life's gradual journey. While often interrupted by other attractions and distractions on the way, it is essentially an ascent to God, with the Divine hidden everywhere on the way, always calling us from the depths of our desire. All Sri Pada's elements contributed to this realization: the fog and rain, the lights illuminating the ascending, irregular path, the bell at the summit summoning pilgrims to the heights — all seemed part of our ultimate, inner journey to wholeness, enlightenment, and divine love.

As my companions and I were nearing the top, I thought pessimistically, "With this fog and drizzle, we'll never be able to see the sun." As we arrived at the summit, I watched as each pilgrim rang the bell the number of times they had climbed Sri Pada. My two friends disappeared in the peak's fortlike maze, and I found myself curiously alone to face the dawn. As I looked out into the thick clouds that obscured its approach, the sun appeared as a slight, pale presence in the midst of the fog, a barely perceptible, ghostly specter. But as I watched, its rays literally melted through the clouds, which then parted, and I found myself face-to-face with the sun. It seemed like more than the sun, however. Something had happened; a sort of mythic dimension had opened, and nature's mythic quality became a vehicle for a mystical experience.

As I stood with the sun on the summit of this modest mountain peak, the solar orb became a catalyst for my encounter with the Divine. As often appears in myths, the sun became the conveyance for God, like a chariot of fire. It ushered me into the Divine Presence through its powerful symbolic function, its archetypal capacity to represent the One. I was overcome as I stood alone before the Divine. I was seized by the Presence communicated through the sudden appearance of the sun. It carried me into an intense awareness of the Divine's utter reality. I knew then why I had made this journey to Sri Pada, and the peace it conveyed remains with me to this day.

Nature's Symbolism

The world, particularly the natural world, contains a symbolic dimension of meaning, a sacramental economy.[4] This symbolic dimension is an archetypal level of reality that affects even our dreams. Mountains, trees, oceans, rivers, fields, birds, spiders, turtles, pets, stars, galaxies, our moon — indeed everything has an intrinsic meaning beyond its physical reality. And *everyone* holds a timeless contemplative capacity to understand this symbolic world, to grasp its inner meanings, the essential patterns that unite all reality. This capacity has been obscured in the last century by our Western preoccupation with frenetic work, scientific analysis, rational discourse, and technology. Intuition has been choked off, especially in men.

The contemplative capacity to discern the natural symbols embedded in our experience of nature is essentially an intuitive ability that everyone has but that few use.

Although most people relate to nature's beauty with enthusiasm and delight, few today understand its deeper symbolic function. Virtually every ancient and medieval culture exercised this capacity, and many Native American, Aboriginal, and African tribal societies still do. This ability to see and know in this natural, contemplative way was called by St Francis's follower, St. Bonaventure, *reading* the Book of Nature, and we can all regain this faculty through spiritual practice. St. Francis of Assisi and St. Bonaventure were both skilled in this kind of sacred reading. Francis once observed: "If your heart were pure then all of nature would be a great book of holy wisdom and sacred doctrine."

No view of the world is complete without including this subtle form of knowing, a kind of illumination that relies on fully developed intuition. I awakened to this capacity in myself very gradually. It began when, as an undergraduate, I visited a monastery in upstate New York. While on a walk in the monastic garden, the prior remarked to me that "flowers are a contemplation in which God is expressing his love for us." Although I heard his words, they took time to sink in. It didn't happen immediately, but when it did, I experienced a sudden irruption of insight, a stream of intense illumination, a holistic apprehension of an entire process of knowing.

It all came together while I was contemplating a rose bush in my front yard in West Hartford, Connecticut. In watching the bush over time, I realized that reality, like the rose, is a process of growth, or unfolding. Just as the rose is more than any one stage of its development — bud, stem, or bloom — so life and reality are more than any one moment of time or experience. What is real is not just its moments of duration but also the totality of the process in its manifestation in time. This insight can comfort us in facing death and disintegration. All nature communicates this truth to us all the time, if we would but pay attention — the attention of the heart, of intuition, of our being to the sacred mystery. Nature constantly teaches us that a larger picture exists than what we see. It compels us to awaken by confronting us with order, design, and perfection everywhere.

A spider weaving its web, the perfect symmetry of a snowflake, the beauty and harmony of the lily, the cosmic quality of trees, the mysterious presence of the wind, the attraction of stillness, the radiance of light, the transparency of fragrances, the flow of water, the movement of leaves, the timeless feeling of some days and nights, the poetry of birds in flight, the transfiguring moments of dawn and sunset, the hypnotic rhythm of the tides — all speak to us of something beyond ourselves, something that transcends our understanding. All point to nature's ability to nourish us aesthetically and psychologically as well as materially.

When I reflect on the natural world and its glorious messages for us, I remember our responsibility to restore and preserve it, to work toward a sustainable future in which the human community lives in harmony with nature. We have a sacred duty to the earth itself, to one another, and to all the other species that inhabit our planet, to live in a state of friendship with the natural world, enhancing its life by simplifying our needs and desires. We are entrusted with the ongoing task of preserving the systems of the biosphere, the aesthetic reality of nature, and the rights of all sentient beings who dwell here with us. We are admonished to make peace with all of them. The safeguarding of the earth is our highest moral priority, and nothing can take precedence over it any longer.

Once we possess the sensitivity, the larger awareness, to

understand and experience the deeper value of nature, and if we have the generosity to strive for its preservation and well-being, we will work untiringly to inform others of the necessity to protect the earth, all species, and also the human species, particularly in its most vulnerable members, the homeless. I will explore in more detail the urgency of the plight of the homeless and our responsibility toward them in chapter 6.

THE WORLD AS COMMUNITY

We are social beings who grow in relation to others; we are defined through our relationships with them. Our ancestors lived their lives in the bosom of a supportive tribe. Every need was met within the context of that tribe. The tribe *was* community. When we moved out of tribes and into extended families, and then into nuclear families, we gained greater freedom and mobility, but something was lost: a fundamental sense of security based on the experience of belonging. We must seek to rediscover and recover community in our lives. Community gives us psychological balance, promotes healthy human development, creates stability in the midst of change, and acts as an anchor that gives us focus and calm — a timeless, restful, and deeply human order. Community also helps us to meet the needs of all for food, shelter, recreation, work, study, sharing the tasks of child rearing, the whole complex of spiritual life. All are supported through the group.

We need to be conscious of the social world, as well as the natural and symbolic worlds, because we have a permanent responsibility to it, to our human family. The social world embraces all relationships, from the most indifferent to the most intimate, and the different contexts in which these relationships unfold. This realm also includes the various communities that bind people together, which allow us to meet and

9

work together for the common good. It is also through these forums that our cultural life develops, and stimulation — whether aesthetic, intellectual, or emotional — is marshaled into creative outlets that give us culture. We produce culture as a way to cocreate our sense of world. We are all engaged in some act of creating culture, a definitively human act.

Our stewardship of the natural world and of the social world are linked, since community plays an indispensable role in the preservation of the earth, the rescuing of other species, and the survival of the human family. We cannot think of the continued existence of the social world as primarily dependent on the nuclear family. We need to identify with a larger, more diverse, and more flexible social organism — the community itself. Religious or spiritual communities provide both the simple experience of community in a world that goes increasingly without it and the support for each individual to pursue his or her journey. Many well-organized religious communities are dedicated to service and prayer, often a contemplative form of prayer. Mother Teresa's Missionaries of Charity are celebrated in this respect. They work in some eighty countries, mostly in urban areas where they aid the poorest of the poor. They embrace a voluntary form of simplicity established in a rhythm of contemplative prayer and tireless work with society's abandoned.

Another beautiful example of viable community is the Foculare, named after the Italian word for hearth. The Foculare are a six-million-member lay Catholic society founded in Trent, Italy, in 1943. The Foculare live in more than a hundred countries. They work in every profession. Some live in intentional communities, while the majority live in families. Whatever their station, they all share in this larger identity, which emphasizes daily prayer, the Eucharist, interfaith encounter, and ecumenical dialogue. Highly educated, they are in the vanguard of positive change around the world.

For ten years, between 1982 and 1992, I lived in New Boston, New Hampshire, at the Hundred Acres Monastery, where I experienced a similar kind of community. Five Trappist monks from Holy Cross Abbey in Berryville, Virginia, founded Hundred Acres (named in the 1700s for the hundred and four acres it sat on) in 1964 as a way to return to monastic simplicity. They also admitted laypeople — men and women, even whole families, and non-Catholics — and most of the time it worked. Hundred Acres was usually a quiet place, and members and a constant flow of guests were given a lot of freedom. The community kept a minimal schedule, with a common dinner in the evening preceded by Mass, which wasn't obligatory. Our life there as a community was one of genuine simplicity. Life centered on basic activities like manual labor, cooking, farming, gardening, chopping and storing wood, cleaning, and writing. We also worked hard to extend hospitality to all guests and strangers through providing retreats and spiritual direction.

The schedule for the few of us who were monastics was informal, and much of the time, solitary. I would rise around 6 A.M. and spend an hour in prayer. Then I'd eat breakfast and work in the community for much of the day, doing such assigned tasks as cooking, collecting the mail, and giving retreats and spiritual direction. I would cook dinner two or three times a week. In the afternoon I'd take the dogs for a walk before engaging in another hour of contemplative prayer. Before dinner we would have Mass. After supper, a few of us would do the dishes, and then the evenings were free. Then some would read, talk a bit, or perhaps watch a movie.

You cannot imagine the peace this little island of contemplation provided, with its exquisite garden in the huge backyard. There was a mysterious presence there, a sacred reality. I would feel it from time to time, especially when I was quietly sitting in the tiny chapel. Though our community was not very well known, it gave so much to so many people in its years of existence. There was love there, not sentimental love, but the depth of what the Catholic tradition calls charity, or the selfless love of the Gospel.

In the late 1980s, the community welcomed five Afghani *mujaheddin*, or freedom fighters, for six months. They were in America receiving medical treatment from their battle wounds, and only one of them spoke English. They had never had any experience of Christians before this, but they grew to love us, and we them. The five would attend Mass every evening, and although they never received Holy Communion, they remained profoundly respectful. I often look back on this encounter during our current turmoil, realizing how centuries of fierce religious divisions melted away through simple human contact. Here is an example of how the living power of community, a nurturing human environment, opened minds and hearts and transformed attitudes.

But most important, as I'll argue throughout this book, community can be found outside the monastery. We can all discover it, whether by becoming more aware of the people around us or in more secular intentional communities, which are more typical of the modern movement toward community. My cousin, Jeanine Colbert Boucher, and her husband, Marc Boucher, live in the Portland, Oregon, area with their two children, whom they adopted from an orphanage in Calcutta: a boy named Anand, meaning joy, and a girl, Pria, which means love. For many years Marc and Jeanine have lived in an intentional community with another couple and their children. They share many activities, including an evening meal, prayer, and a weekly Mass. Marc, a poet, was an organic farmer, and Jeanine worked in health care. They belonged to a larger, loosely organized community of some thirty socially conscious and environmentally committed people. They all lived in their own homes but did many things together each month and took yearly retreats in the country.

Community can take many forms, depending on the situations of those who undertake its challenging work and commitment. Whatever form it does take, for it to work, financial arrangements and obligations have to be clearly defined and the community's work fairly distributed. Although it is clearly not necessary, a common spiritual focus can make this process happen more smoothly. Striving for a common goal, with shared philosophy and values, can make the difficulties of living with others easier. Yet one definition of true community is that it includes individuals who are difficult or even abhorrent. And here is our true challenge as mystics in the world: to create community with those who are so different from us that we feel we have nothing in common with them. As our world becomes smaller, through a growing common culture, the true test of community will be our tolerance for our most profound differences and love for the most challenging among us.

THE WORLD AS TESTING GROUND

As a monk living in the city, I am always aware that the world can be a dangerous place. We must develop a precise perspective about the nature of the dangers the world presents. We are all faced with all kinds of temptation. It was in remote regions of the deserts of Syria, Palestine, and Egypt that the desert fathers and mothers were put to the test, that they did battle with the demons. The desert was a place of trial and of testing our mettle as contemplatives dedicated to God. Now, in our age, the desert is in the city — that is, in civilization. Whether we live in sprawling suburbs or rural communities, we're all tied together by the common culture of technology, in an increasingly confusing and complicated world.

This world is a very exciting place. There is so much to see and experience, to learn, share, and remember. At the same time there is so much to avoid and to be wary of — so much that could compromise the spiritual and moral primacy to which our lives must be dedicated. The early Christian Church knew that the city was the place of sin, of intense temptation, but also of victory over self. For Antony of Egypt, the father of Christian monasticism, it is said that this victory came by divine possession, that is, when "wholly possessed by the Spirit of God, who has driven out of him once and for all the spirit of evil and his illusions."[5] Because of this victory over self, Antony had no fear of the city or the world.[6]

The mystic must face the negative possibilities of sin — the temptations that everyone living actively in society must face every day. Sin is selfishness, and we must accept a sense of solidarity with all people, realizing that they need us, and we need to be part of their struggles, their hopes, fears, and dreams. For this reason we live in the world. There is, in our age, a special need for mystics to be present in the world. Their insight, dedication to contemplation, and their heart are needed by those who seek ultimate wholeness, joy, and inner peace, all of which come from living a spiritual life.

The world, especially the city, also offers opportunities for our own growth in love, mercy, compassion, kindness, and sensitivity. We see need everywhere. It glares at us in the desperate violence of the ghettos, where drive-by shootings are commonplace; in the endless need for tutors and mentors; in the constant abuse of drugs and other vices; in the forgotten elderly; in the brutal disconnection from nature's beauty. Everywhere we see opportunities for compassion, for letting go of self-preoccupation in the spontaneous act of responding to the immense suffering we constantly encounter. A contemplative in the heart of the world has the opportunity to be aware of, to relate to, to touch and heal this suffering, to be a sign of love and hope to those who are so vulnerable in this difficult and indifferent world.

Let us again consider the example of Mother Teresa and her Missionaries of Charity. This active contemplative — with her own hands — retrieved and saved 42,000 people, picking them up from the streets of Calcutta, carrying them to her home for the dying. Although so much more can be done by governments and organizations to transform the systematic causes of such suffering, vulnerability, and marginality, there is no guarantee that anything can be wakened in the masses without such heroic examples of holiness. This love in action is the personal work every one of us must do, and it is the most vital contribution a mystic can make to his or her brothers and sisters living out active lives in society. And because the mystic is a person of prayer, of contemplative meditation, of mystical life in the hiddenness and anonymity of the city's turmoil, he or she is able to make this contribution.

Countless souls, without the celebrity of a saint like Mother Teresa, go about their lives of holiness and joy, being present to and responding to those who suffer, from a vast reservoir of peace that arises as the fruit of contemplation. There is no other way they could do it. For these extraordinary beings, the world — whatever part they inhabit — represents a golden opportunity to *be* love in action, perhaps never noticed by anybody but nonetheless effective and profoundly valuable in the lives of others.

We must recognize that vulnerability and need are not only material. Mother Teresa often said that the greater poverty is loneliness. One can also add the incapacity or unwillingness to love. People caught in that sort of malaise require the inspiration and examples of mystics among us. The world — and all of life — offers us the opportunity for transformation by giving us occasions to transcend ourselves. The opportunity is everywhere. I realize more and more that I am needed in this work of transformation in the heart of our planet's busyness, needed precisely as a hermit monk going about my prayer and work where most people live. For me, it is a constant call to surrender to God, to Christ, or the Divine present in everyone and in every situation. Although we can become mired in self-preoccupation, it is important to realize that no distinction exists between the sacred and profane. Everything is sacred!

Perhaps one day we will witness the eventual emergence of a universal order of *sannyasis:* contemplatives or mystics from all traditions united in their awareness, their love, and their dedication to the earth, humankind, and all sentient beings. (I will discuss this phenomenon at greater length in chapter 9.) As mystics in the world, are we not creating this universal order? Do we not thereby become natural advocates for the homeless, the poor, the marginalized, the oppressed, the starving, the diseased? Are we not allies of the natural world in its struggle to be and to seek harmony with the human species? This universal order has the pressing task of raising the consciousness of the world, to that highest level to which Ken Wilber often refers and to which all the great spiritual paths are dedicated.

What informs my contemplation, and the action that flows forth from it, is the urgent, always present realization of our essential interdependence, our interconnectedness. My Catholic tradition and the wider Christian community call it the Mystical Body of Christ. Buddhism names it "dependent arising." Science

verifies it as the unity of the cosmos in an underlying intercon-
necting web of relationships. There is only one reality, in which
we arise and transcend. Nothing stands outside this one cosmic
system of life in which we all participate. I believe the Spirit is
calling us to realize this truth, to allow ourselves to be transformed by it, and so, to transform the world.

CHAPTER 2

Intimacy with the Divine

Spiritual Practice and Mystical Experience

In a wonderful Hindu story, a man tells his friend about an extraordinary spiritual teacher he has met. Although his friend is curious about this teacher, he is also somewhat skeptical, so he decides to seek out this holy man and put him to the test. After asking around, he discovers the master is living and teaching nearby, so the young man goes to see him and manages to obtain an audience with him. He defiantly walks before the teacher, and before he can catch himself, blurts out a challenge: "Show me God! Prove to me that he exists!"

The saintly master calmly extends his hand and, in a soothing, inviting tone, says, "Come with me." The young person takes the teacher's hand, in the Asian sign of friendship, and off they go to the neighborhood beach. As they reach the ocean, the teacher leads the man into the surf and tells him to dive into the water. Then the master does something even stranger. He holds the man's head under the water. As the minutes pass, the man tries three times to come up, but the guru holds his head firmly submerged. Finally, on his fourth attempt, the teacher lets him out of the water. The poor soul bursts out of the water, gasping for air. "What are you trying to do, kill me?" he yells at the saint. The holy man looks at him with infinite compassion and lovingly, patiently responds: "Forgive me if I caused you undue anxiety, but when your desire for God is as desperate as your desire for air, for your very breath, then you will find God!"

This powerful story dramatically illustrates the importance of commitment in the spiritual life. No genuine progress is possible without it. Such a commitment expresses itself in the discipline of regular, daily spiritual practice that paves the way for breakthroughs, for the miracles of grace to happen.

Spiritual practice is the core of our transformation, and it requires what can be called the contemplative attitude, a disposition to a life of mystical depth. Spiritual practice often means meditation and other forms of inner exploration. It can also mean prayer. Silence, solitude, and mysticism — the seeking of illumination and wisdom — are further parts of the contemplative experience, a process of our ultimate evolution, our unfolding to higher states of consciousness. To understand how this process can unfold in our lives, we need to explore its elements.

THE CONTEMPLATIVE ATTITUDE

The mystic — the person who directly experiences Ultimate Reality, the Divine, or vast consciousness — although living in the midst of the world's busyness is anchored in an indescribable peace, a joy that cannot be apprehended by the hard secular mentality that, at its worst, is addicted to thoughtless, banal pursuits, immersed in ceaseless entertainment and the constant hunt for more and more things. Our culture is burdened by a steady stream of chatter that reflects a noisy mind and a cluttered heart. At the same time, it is possible to live a secular life of integrity and quality, depth and creativity. Although I have certainly been caught up in this inner frenzy and outer activity, I feel lucky to have discovered fairly early, around age nineteen or twenty, the contemplative dimension of life and experience.

This dimension is first known as a way of relating to all things: the cosmos, the natural world, society, others, God, and oneself in the Divine. We relate on a deeper level of attention. Paradoxically, we are alert while resting in the depth of attention. It is not a passive observing but a commitment to being aware of the divine mystery enveloping everything. It is love, our love for God, that animates the contemplative attitude, just as it is divine love that inspires, guides, nourishes, and maintains contemplation. There are two sides to this love: ours and the Divine's. The contemplative attitude is already the active reality of the mystical life at work in us, and this Presence is the Divine itself.

The disposition of contemplative attention, the decision to follow this path and live by such a precious wisdom seeking, is the foundation of being a monk, or mystic, in the world. The person with a contemplative attitude, whose life is shaped by its demanding discipline, shows a wonderful sensitivity to everyone and everything. It is a sensitivity born out of an awakened capacity for union with God. Everything, every person and situation, becomes an occasion for communion with the mystery in the silence of the heart. Alert, attentive, receptive, and responsive, the contemplative person is awake to the possibility of communion with the Source in every action.

Being *in* the world but not *of* it characterizes the contemplative attitude. How can anyone truly be of the world — that is, be totally influenced by its values — if he or she knows there is something infinitely more real and urgent? The mystic not only knows there is more, but he or she actually becomes more conscious of it, experiencing it daily. The contemplative attitude is about seeing, and the nature of this seeing, its "object" if you like, is precisely this infinite more — the ground of all that is.

How do we attain a contemplative attitude? Through daily spiritual practice, which requires total commitment to regular prayer or spiritual practice. This commitment takes many forms, as we shall discover, but in practical terms it translates into an assiduous practice pursued in an environment of quiet, peace, rest, or stillness. In time, spiritual practice *becomes* this atmosphere of peace, rest, inner stillness and outer quiet, or rather it becomes closely identified with it. The contemplative attitude is cultivated through deep attention to what is before us; it requires an intention to seek and be receptive to the Divine wherever we may be, wherever we may look. It is a passion for the subtle reality of the Presence, the Divine Presence, that awakens this capacity in us.

Since I was a teenager I have sought the mystical life. I think this pursuit began for me in earnest when the example of St. Francis of Assisi began to influence my young life, and I would devote time each day for private prayer. Later, it deepened and expanded through contemplative or mystical meditation. For me, the contemplative attitude developed organically out of my spiritual life when I became serious about prayer. The intensity, depth, and breadth of prayer initiated me into not only contemplation itself but also into a wider contemplative attitude that slowly enveloped my life. It is never merely a fleeting mystical experience; it is the whole interior disposition that makes such fleeting experiences possible. As I developed a twice-daily habit of centering prayer, a Christian form of meditation, a contemplative attitude emerged quite naturally in my awareness.

As this way of seeing, experiencing, and knowing — also a form of illumination, feeling, and intuition — dawned in my life, everything opened to my understanding through an inner gaze of attentiveness. The perfection of certain flowers, the flight of birds, the movement of trees and clouds, the magnificent heights of mountains, the smiles of children, the laughter of friends, the rhythmic cadence of the sea, the fragile beauty of butterflies — all these and countless other details of the world revealed their secrets through contemplation.

The contemplative attitude can also be born in you when you take the time to notice these compelling instances of spirit, and many more, manifested in nature, being, and life. One of the most fundamental ways to be a mystic in the world is to give yourself the time each day to appreciate what is always before you. Contemplation begins with what the English mystical tradition calls "a long, loving look at the real." The contemplative attitude is a very natural way of knowing when we understand the value of silence, the quiet, and stillness. As we develop the habit of noticing, of deep looking, then instances of epiphany in the natural world and daily life take us more and more into contemplation. The contemplative attitude is our preparation for the gift of contemplation itself, while contemplation is the experience of the Divine Presence and union with it.

By developing this capacity to look and see in a long, steady, loving way, the attitude of contemplation takes root as a deep habit of being. Once awakened, the contemplative attitude must be cultivated each day, and it must never be taken for granted.

SPIRITUAL PRACTICE IN THE CITY

My life of prayer contains many elements: contemplative meditation, *lectio divina;* the practice of nature, including walking meditation and sky meditation; contemplative study and reflection; and allowing for silence and solitude. It sounds complicated, but it is simply what I have found to work after years of experience. While I live in a big American city and my spiritual observance is carried on there, I keep to these practices wherever I am. I make allowances for flexibility, depending on my schedule as it follows work and travel, but I remain faithful to these practices wherever I may find myself.

Contemplative Meditation

The heart of my daily practice is contemplative meditation. It is more formally known as centering prayer, as developed by Father Thomas Keating, and though it's not called contemplation it leads to it in time, facilitating its growth and evolution.[1] I have discovered the capacity of centering prayer to lead to mystical contemplation during years of sitting quietly before, in, and surrounded by the Divine Presence. The breakthrough to contemplation has come from the Divine's initiative rather than from my effort. For my part, I simply continue my faithfulness to prayer.

How meditation became contemplation for me has everything to do with grace, or the Divine's action in me.[2] I say this because my mind, like a chattering monkey, to use an Indian image, throughout the years has been distressingly active in prayer, and especially in centering prayer. Our minds are active by nature, but my mind is profoundly so, since my training as a theologian tends to encourage a lot of thinking. It's an occupational requirement of a philosopher to think, I suppose, but in meditation it can become a serious obstacle.

I experienced tremendous difficulty in my early years of practice. This difficulty came from my habit of thinking too much, and not surrendering, not letting go of the mind's control. At times it seemed hopeless, and I often felt like a failure, but I never gave up. And sure enough, my patience was finally rewarded, and something truly extraordinary happened one morning in October 1982 as I sat peacefully in meditation in the tiny chapel of my New Hampshire monastery. I began the meditation session with the usual distraction of endless thoughts. But after a few minutes something shifted, and I experienced a dramatic change. Although I was still thinking, a deeper reality was emerging, or I was simply becoming more aware of it. I found myself being carried by an immense, all-encompassing Presence. My meditation had transformed into contemplation, or mystical prayer, where before it had just been centering prayer, with moments of profound peace and a passing sense of God's presence.

When we are awake in a contemplative sense, each moment draws us more into the Divine Presence. Divine grace communicated itself to me; a new and direct manner of experiencing God had surfaced in my life. Reaching this kind of experience required me to work on meditative practice each day. Centering Prayer is meant to awaken us to the reality of the Divine beyond the usual operations of the mind; it provided me a pervading atmosphere of God's presence and action in the depths of my being, in my understanding — even in the psychological dynamics of my character and in my capacity to respond to others.

To make this possible, after you settle comfortably and close your eyes, you introduce a sacred word, sacred because it represents our decision to give ourselves to God. When we are overcome by thoughts or preoccupations while practicing, the method asks us to return gently to the sacred word, which becomes a vehicle for reaching deeper states of interior quiet.

Finally, centering prayer counsels a careful transition from the actual period of prayer back to ordinary consciousness. It calls for a few minutes to make the transition through a verbal prayer like the Our Father or another prayer appropriate to the tradition of the practitioner.

Usually I can do two forty-five minute periods of meditation a day — one in the early morning, the other in the late afternoon or early evening. Sometimes a third becomes possible at midday.

Lectio Divina

Between these periods of contemplative centering prayer, I engage in *lectio divina,* or spiritual reading. Although it's not always possible to fit it in, it usually happens one way or another, sufficient to my needs.[3] *Lectio divina* is an ancient monastic practice of contemplation that nourishes our lives. For me, *lectio divina* is one of the most powerful ways to remove myself from the corrupting influence of the modern world. In its early history as a form of prayer, it focused primarily on meditative reading of scripture or the life of a saint. In more recent centuries, in addition to scripture, *lectio divina* has drawn on the writings of mystics and saints, and even theological works. Like centering prayer, *lectio* is a kind of prayer designed to provide a context in which contemplation will develop.

Reaching contemplation naturally unfolds in four stages or acts each time we engage in *lectio.* Beginning with a text, we read very slowly, not concerned with information but simply with allowing the Spirit to ignite inspiration in us. Once this happens, we stop and enter the second stage, that of reflection. Reflection does not mean analysis. Rather, it's an intuitive probing of that part of the text or event that has sparked the inspiration. Here we troll for the depth and roots of the inspiration, the deeper meanings hidden in the text. It's a process of assimilation that reaches a point of satiation; when it does, we then pass into the third stage of *lectio,* called affective prayer.

Affective prayer, the prayer of the heart, engages our feelings and emotions. It's a stirring of our love for God, an intense, highly focused movement of the will toward the Divine in an act of self-donation. It represents an intensification of our affections, a magnification of our capacity to express our love for God. *The Cloud of Unknowing,* the fourteenth-century mystical classic by an anonymous Carthusian monk, refers to it as "a blind stirring of love." And "it is nothing else than a sudden impulse, one that comes without warning, speedily flying up to God as the spark flies up from the burning coal."[4] It is the Divine Lover who effects this love within our hearts. As this love reaches its completion, we enter the fourth stage, that of contemplation itself.

Contemplation, in the tradition of *lectio,* is through and through experiential. It is about actually knowing God intimately in this high degree of prayer and consciousness. It is your direct awareness and my direct awareness of the Ultimate Reality that cannot be contained or known by our minds in a conceptual way. Contemplation awakens in us the capacity to be directly aware of God, and it is God who triggers this awareness in us.

This fourth stage of *lectio,* along with the preceding three, occurs quite spontaneously, though shaped by the influence of grace, at least in my experience. There is nothing inflexible about the movement up and down the four rungs of *lectio divina.* We move quite naturally from one level to the next. The process unfolds spontaneously each time we engage in this type of prayer, and each session may be as short as thirty to forty-five minutes and as long as two or three hours.

The Practice of Nature

Another fundamental part of my spiritual practice is a daily, hour-long walk. But it isn't just a walk; it's a contemplative experience I call the practice of nature. Others call it walking meditation or walking contemplation. It is much more vigorous than a Buddhist walking meditation but has a similar purpose. However we name it, what it offers is the same: a communion with nature and the Divine while walking. It has assumed great importance in my life, and I cannot conceive of my life without it. It has become an endless source of insight, inspiration, and of course necessary physical exercise. Nature, and the Divine immanent in all things, conveys so much wisdom.[5] I become open to this wisdom by a kind of active receptivity practiced while walking.

I often say the rosary as I'm walking, and this has also become contemplation for me. This ancient devotion not only connects me with my tradition but also with the other religions that have their own version of the rosary, such as *mala* beads of the Hindus and the Buddhists, or the beads of the Muslims. I have said the rosary all my life, even while I lived in India, and so embracing this devotion allows me a measure of continuity with my earlier practice of prayer. I have found that reciting the prayers of the rosary has a mantric quality that gradually leads me into a contemplative state, while in vital connection with the natural about you as you walk.

Another dimension of the practice of nature is sky meditation, a Tibetan practice that helps to give us a subtle sense of our own nature — both the mind and heart. In this meditative practice, one simply gets comfortable and relaxed — important requirements — and then gazes at the sky for roughly fifteen minutes. Fairly quickly, the vastness of the sky — both as a metaphor and a physical reality — mirrors back the vastness of our own being. Our consciousness is as immense as the heavens above. Our hearts are equally vast in their capacity for love, kindness, compassion, mercy, and sensitivity. Sky meditation uses the image of the heavens, or a natural reality, to achieve a spiritual and psychological realization. It is a powerful tool of inner awakening.

Contemplative Study and Reflection

Without fail, I allot sufficient time each week for contemplative study and reflection. These activities also nourish my contemplative life and are always done within this context, even when they relate to my work of teaching, lecturing, writing, and giving retreats. Again, these activities connect with earlier periods of my life, those years when I was a student. I am able to process information, insight, and life itself through reading, study, and reflection, integrating all three within myself and relating them to my own spiritual journey. My studies and reflection range over theology, the sacred texts of various traditions, philosophy, works in spirituality, politics, monastic literature, science, and popular literature, even science fiction.

Allowing for Silence

The context and environment of the mystic in the city, in the heart of society, are silence and solitude. They are my constant companions, fellow travelers on the spiritual journey, and eloquently wise teachers of the hidden inner path. It would be very difficult, if not impossible, to be a contemplative — whether in the city, the monastery, or some remote hermitage — without the benefit of these two precious resources and primary values of mystical life. Solitude is the teacher and silence is the teaching. We need both in order to grow.

Silence and stillness — the *quies* or *hesychia* of the desert tradition, the quiet of heart, mind, and will — is an extremely important asset in developing intimacy with God. I remember so well how this precious knowledge was introduced to me many years ago, when Thomas Keating said to me: "Silence is God's language, and it's a very difficult language to learn." In many ways, my contemplative practice, especially meditation or centering prayer, is concerned with gaining proficiency, depth, and comfort in this "language." Over the years, with considerable effort and commitment, this divine tongue has become second nature to me. It became familiar and easy only when I learned to submit to it, allowing its restfulness to take hold of my being and attention.

To say that God's language is silence is to suggest that the Divine Reality itself is silence or stillness. The desert fathers and mothers of the early church and followers of the monastic tradition have always known the value of silence. Many centuries ago, they took to heart the words of The Eternal One in Psalm 46: "Be still, and you will know that I am God," which means, "If you'd learn to be quiet and still, you would discover that I Am."[6] You would experience that I, your God, actually exists, and you would know with certitude that I am real, that God exists and is existence itself.

Silence is really an open secret, as older, wiser people seem to prefer it, while young folks often don't yet understand it. When I was a teenager, my Uncle John would repeat to me the need to cultivate silence. My uncle was partly referring to the social dimension of silence as self-protection, a way of keeping others guessing. But he was also aware of its spiritual qualities and its meaning as the bond between those who love each other.

As we develop and maintain our spiritual lives, silence becomes like that rare "pearl of great price" mentioned in the Gospel. It is at once a means of deeper awareness of God's Presence and the sheer evidence that we have found God. It is very subtle in the pervasive way it hides, or veils, the Presence. To unveil this mysterious Presence simply requires that we cultivate deep spiritual attentiveness — a listening heart, being, will, and imagination. Each of these faculties becomes engaged creatively in this kind of attentiveness. The heart is attentive through its growing capacity for love; we listen with our being by allowing ourselves to be present to God; the will pays attention to and is aware of a direction by intending the Divine; the imagination "listens" to the images that arise from our contact with the world around us.

An attentive, listening attitude and practice lead to deeper levels of interior silence and stillness. This capacity for silence has five degrees: silence of speech, thought, will, the unconscious, and being. They unfold quite naturally as we respond to the call to go farther, a call that will integrate the insight and truth of stillness in all dimensions of our common human being.

The silence of speech. The silence of speech is important and obvious. It is only by disciplining our desire for talk that we become aware of an omnipresent reality behind the chatter. As we master our tongues, we experience a pervasive peace and a freedom from compulsive speech and then behavior. But the silence of speech, and the disciplining of our tendency to talk, is a sign of, and an invitation to, a more profound silence: that of mind, or thought.

The silence of thought. The silence of thought aims at quieting the near ceaseless mental chatter, the stream of consciousness as one thought succeeds another. Meditation — particularly nondiscursive modes that don't involve thought but transcend thinking altogether — is designed to bring the peace of a quiet mind and a mental faculty resting in God. It takes years to learn this degree of silence, because it goes against our natural propensity. Like birds talking in trees as sunset approaches, our minds chatter endlessly within us. Meditation and sleep provide our only relief. But the silence of the mind is also a sign of and invitation to, a more ultimate degree of inner quiet: that of the will.

The silence of will. Whereas speech is only an external activity and some thought brings peace to our mental sphere, silence of the will takes the process to a psychological and moral depth not readily grasped in our culture, with its understanding of freedom as the capacity to will what you want and do as you like. To draw the will, each of our wills, to stillness of desire is not easy. Stillness of will is really detachment from desire, or at least selfish desires. It means having a nonpossessive attitude in all areas of our lives, to be freed from a bondage to passions, to avoid allowing our desires to lead or shape us. Silence of the will is a contemplative achievement; it is something the Spirit provides if we ask for it, choose it, and work hard to maintain it.

Silence of the will requires a further degree of interior quiet, that of the silence of the unconscious. We cannot hope to quiet desire — especially selfish desire — unless we can get at the roots of the passions in their unconscious source. Since many desires have their seeds in the unconscious, we are called to an even deeper level of interior quiet, that of our unconscious life.

The silence of the unconscious. This focus of stillness takes a lot of work and grace. It cannot be achieved without persistent divine assistance, for it is God who works and acts in us to heal the roots of desire and the wounds of earlier experience. Part of the process of contemplation is precisely the elimination in the unconscious of desires that compete for God's attention.

And yet even when the stillness of the unconscious dawns for us, there remains a final degree or stage of silence, what can be called the silence of being itself.

The silence of being. This silence of being means that every obstacle between the Divine and us has disappeared, overcome by the power and determination of God's love in us. In terms of our nature and God's, it is as if there is only God and God's eternal being. Our being is taken up in God's.

Each of these degrees of silence works in tandem toward the greater good of our development into a permanent union with God. This permanent condition of union, and every stage in between, or on the way, depends on divine grace, and is, in my experience, pure gift. In this sense, stillness is the doorway to Being, to that which is ultimately real, the entrance into the fullness of the mystical life, that of the joys of union with God. Without this kind of stillness, the Divine Presence is barely perceptible. Perhaps this is one reason, in the Taoist tradition, it is observed: "Stillness is the greatest revelation!"

Embracing Solitude

It can be said that solitude is the teacher, and silence is the teaching. Solitude provides an environment for life with God. In my experience, it is like a warm greenhouse in which the relationship grows and eventually flowers. It is also like a matrix containing, or housing, my relationship with God. In this sense, solitude contains, or becomes a vehicle of, my contemplative awareness. My solitary hermitage allows contemplation to expand from the inner privacy and hiddenness of my heart to the container, the matrix that solitude offers. Solitude, then, is a sacred place consecrated both by a person's intention and by the generosity of the Divine. Together they form a marriage out of the pure desire for mystical union and a transforming communion. Contemplation mysteriously extends itself to fill this sacred dwelling where I have decided to be in love with God. Although I cannot speak for other hermit monks, I believe it is the same for them, and it can surely be true of any person who cultivates solitude.

The Divine Consciousness makes a home with us, not simply in our hearts or in the depths of our subjectivity, but in every nook and cranny of our actual home. Everything becomes charged with the Divine's Presence and energy. This awareness is an enduring and palpable experience for me and is powerfully reinforced in silence, which allows it to emerge in bold relief. I am overwhelmingly conscious of the Divine as containing, and maintaining, this place and of the Divine's admitting me into the holy sanctuary of solitude's secret chamber, a sacred precinct to which only the Spirit can grant entrance. The Divine has taken my solitude, in its physical, external form and fashioned it into a sacred temple for God's Holy Spirit and myself to dwell in intimacy and divine peace.

I have come to realize more and more how silence fills solitude, while solitude permits God to fill us. We need to cultivate inner stillness and quiet to actualize the depth of this realization in us, to ignite it into a blazing, glorious, and permanent fruit of contemplation itself. It is only in silence, in the spirit of interior quiet, or in the calm of nonpossessiveness and nongrasping, that we become aware of the possibility of being with God in a kind of spiritual marriage.

A place of solitude becomes the mystical chamber of the person and the divine Beloved. Stillness and silence draw attention to the sacredness of place, because that is where God infallibly dwells, as well as in our deepest subjectivity, the depths of our hearts. Something happens in solitude that rarely occurs in community: We discern, or rather experience, the Divine Presence in an unmistakable way. We discover who is always there with us. We often avoid this looking within, this bare confrontation with who we really are, taking false refuge in the busyness around us.

The supreme value of solitude is that it makes this discovery possible and allows contemplation to unfold in our inner life. Because solitude is the place of intimacy with God, its value is precious beyond all telling. For society, solitude's value is in the perspective it offers and in its contrast with the shallow values of the world. It challenges these superficial values with the pure gold of contemplative wisdom. Solitude and silence stand as sentinels of a heavenly world mingling, as St. Augustine saw, with this earthly city here below.

MYSTICAL EXPERIENCES: "SPIRATION" AND ILLUMINATION

Prayer, and all the aspects of a disciplined spiritual practice, particularly those with an emphasis on silence and solitude, meditation, and self-denial (not focusing on oneself), has led to important breakthroughs in my spiritual life. These breakthroughs have presented themselves in the guise of intense mystical experiences.

I experience the Divine Presence in many ways, but the form most often available to me is "spiration," or the act of breathing in which the Spirit often manifests itself and communicates itself. This process has given rise to the experience of inspiration, or in-spiration, in which the Spirit breathes into us. To be aware of God through spiration is to become conscious of God's subtle Presence through our own breathing.

My first experience of this communication of God's Spirit occurred in 1982 while I was praying early one morning in the monastic chapel of my monastery. As I sat, I was suddenly seized by an urgent perception of a spirating, or breathing Presence all around me. It filled the whole space of the chapel and beyond; it was all-encompassing, surrounding me. It had the rhythmic cadence of the ocean, with its measured ebb and flow, while also always resting in itself. As I became completely absorbed in the divine spiration, I realized that the Divine Spirit was breathing me into existence. Everything was arising from its perpetual act of spiration; my own act of breathing, my own breath, was borrowed from its perfect breathing in and out. We all share in that eternal spiration of the Spirit. When I am sufficiently absorbed in this experience of divine spiration I realize inwardly my dependence, and that of all beings, on this subtle action of the Source.

A few years later, I discovered resonances of this spiritual phenomenon in a number of sacred texts from different traditions and in the works of certain mystics. In the Rig Veda, one of the most ancient Hindu texts, we find a reference to spiration. Speaking in the context of eternity, and before the creation, the author of this Veda remarks: "The One breathed without breath, by its own impulse."[7] The Bible refers to God's Spirit as the *ruah,* the divine wind, or breath, hovering over the primordial waters of chaos.[8] At the creation of man, or Adam, God "blew the breath of life into his nostrils, and man became a living being."[9] Jesus is said to have imparted his Holy Spirit by breathing on his disciples.[10] In *Living Flame of Love* by the sixteenth-century Spanish mystic John of the Cross, I discovered a direct reference to my own experience in contemplation. John of the Cross calls it a spiration in the soul produced by God, imparting knowledge of the Godhead, while increasing the soul's love for him.[11]

Whether I'm in meditation or during the course of the day, a mystical joy often erupts in my heart. Its mysterious appearance and disappearance suggests its divine character and origin. This joy, when it is supernatural, is actually divine grace pouring into my being, and its effects often linger for days at a time. Such joy stirs my love for God and for all beings. It carries me to heights of surrender and peace. When I experience this joy, I often receive spiritual insights that very clearly represent more than my own effort at reflection and thought can produce. Receiving these insights is inspiration, a gift given out of the generosity of the Spirit. It is unmistakable when it happens, and its creative fruits are lasting.

A significant example of inspiration for me was the writing of my last book, *The Mystic Heart.* At every creative stage of the book, from its inception, each session at the computer, to reviewing the final edits, I felt a flood of inspiration as soon as I would consecrate and rededicate the work to God for the benefit of all sentient beings. Each time I made or renewed this intention, a clarity, depth, and vision would take over, and I would give myself over to them. More immediately, this same inspiration is guiding me as I write this book. Whenever this happens, I accept it, as I discern its source and allow it to do the work.

At times I receive intuitive flashes about people, information, my inner experience, and my relationship with God. It even happens in brainstorming sessions for the various organizations to which I belong. For example, I constantly have intuitive insights into the hearts of people, what they are going through, and what they may need. I seem to know these things without effort. I take no credit for this. Indeed, we all experience these flashes to greater or lesser extents. Contemplation simply opens the door much wider and gives me a different way to look at these gifts of wisdom. It helps me experience this illumination and realize it as a process of holistic perception that results from grace.

UNITIVE EXPERIENCE

The highest, most mature form of contemplative, mystical consciousness is unitive experience. The mystics of each tradition have described it in considerable detail. Whether it is the *advaita* of Hinduism, the *satori* of Zen, the *dzogchen* of Tibetan esoteric experience, the *baqa* of the Sufis, or the transforming union of Christian mystics, this high state of awareness is known by all traditions. This is a very important part — a defining integrative awareness — of my own mystical experience.

Many times throughout my years of meditation, in coming out of a session with a group, my perception of others is dramatically altered. I notice something completely extraordinary. Rather than perceiving these people as completely separate from me, as I normally do, I feel that difference disappear; I realize that no differences exist between and among us, that we are united in a deeper, ineffable reality. Although I perceive us as distinct, all sense of separation is gone.

Another way to express this perception is to say that distance is overcome. There is no real sense of distance between these people and me. Much of the separation that seems to exist is cultural and psychological, determined by our socialization. Time and space fold into unity, and I experience others — and, I hope, they me — in a timeless, spaceless now, an immediacy of the real ground of love from which we are always coming forth and to which we are returning. It is an incredibly beautiful, organic, peaceful state.

Whenever I encounter this awareness, I am glimpsing the nature of being and reality, a perception of true existence. This is essential reality, when we become freed from our cultural conditioning and our usual space-time lens. These perceptions express the undivided awareness of original being. When Christian contemplatives view this mystical reality of undivided, nondual consciousness, it is called the transforming union, the mystical marriage between God and the soul. In the unitive experience, the person is united with a personal, loving God.

What has nourished my mystical life are numerous and intense unitive experiences at the Divine's initiative. In these encounters, mysteriously offered to me unexpected and undeserved, the Divine Lover has invaded me, completely affecting every aspect of my being — my mind, will, memory, imagination, unconscious, body, sexuality, and emotions. Overwhelmed by God's invading Presence, I am saturated by the Divine's energies, its subtle actions within me, its intense but measured power. When immersed in union with God, ravished by the Divine's self-giving Presence, overcome in its inpouring love, and elevated into its vast mystery, I am unable to analyze, imagine, remember, or visualize. I can only be receptive, saying yes to God's extraordinary gift. Becoming more actively present to God, I can offer myself in the communion of love to this mysterious God, who remains always the *Deus absconditus,* the hidden God.

THE MYSTICAL PROCESS

The spiritual life, in its fullest sense, as I've observed it in my own life, is a mystical process. It begins when we accept the invitation to live our lives from the deep wells of wisdom, from the depth of transformative or mystical consciousness. This is not an easy matter; it takes commitment and discipline that will span the rest of our earthly sojourn.

The mystical process encompasses several crucial factors of growth, which are continually working together. These include prayer or spiritual practice, living the virtues, compassionate action in all aspects of life, and the work of integration, which involves cleansing the unconscious of its seeds of selfish desire and intention. As a Christian, I am also aware that grace plays a decisive role in the process, and as St. Augustine understood, we cannot even desire God, or embrace the spiritual journey, unless divine grace inspires us. Prayer and spiritual practice are synonymous in my personal understanding; both are forms of each other.

Accompanying our efforts, and the contribution of grace in our mystical development, must be a total commitment to following the guidance of the virtues, like faith, hope, love, patience, gentleness, courage, generosity, and joy. These extend the divine life *within* us to those *around* us, and their practice has lasting effects on others and on us. They become transformative habits placing us on the path to perfection, which is always a path and never a destination reached in this life. The peace, calm, joy, love, and the Divine Presence, which are so available during contemplative meditation, can find expression in our practice of the virtues as well, and the virtues make our ordinary life consistent with our inner, transformative experience.

The practice of the virtues also means the practice of mercy, compassion, kindness, sensitivity, and love in our daily encounters with others. It requires that these virtues be more than deeply held attitudes, more than theoretical guides of behavior, but integral actions, guiding how our behavior takes shape in the real world. They take root in our identity, our character, and our being as we move through this distracted culture in search of integration with the ultimate mystery. We can discern the reality of such integral practice of the virtues in figures like Mother Teresa, Mairead Maguire, Thomas Keating, the Dalai Lama, and Desmond Tutu. But it is also evident in millions of other people who are unknown, yet just as heroic, in their practical virtue.

In tandem with praying and upholding the virtues is the arduous work of inner transformation that comes through the self-knowledge that surfaces for us in prayer. Contemplation always exposes our hidden motivations in our unconscious memory of our early life or even of more recent experiences, it gives us lucid realizations of our inner states, and it grants us sobering self-knowledge.

We realize the need to cleanse ourselves of the seeds of selfishness and negativity and to permit the unconscious to integrate with our deepest intention for God and love. This process takes time and requires that we actively participate by renewing our intention and attention. If the unconscious remains unintegrated with our spiritual lives because these seeds continue to grow into our conscious experience, then we have a divided heart, a will desiring God but other goods as well. We cannot have it both ways. When Jesus said, "You cannot serve two masters," he didn't mean that we can't desire other things but that we shouldn't prefer them to God. To become integrated, we need to pull out these unconscious roots and surrender them to the higher order of divine love. When we do, the unconscious is united with the conscious and the superconscious — the Divine — and they all work together for our complete transformation.

DREAMS, READING HEARTS, CLAIRVOYANCE, AND DIVINE PROTECTION

One night in June 1985, while I was living at Hundred Acres Monastery, I had a dream about Bede Griffiths's ashram in Tamil Nadu, India. In the dream I was sitting on the floor with Father Bede and the theologian Raimon Panikkar in some strange, open-air building. I had never been there before, yet the dream was strangely real, filled with details of the structure's construction and atmosphere. More than a year later, in November 1986, I began a six-month stay at Shantivanam with Father Bede. At Christmas, Panikkar mysteriously showed up without warning and stayed for a few days. On the second day of his visit, Panikkar gave a fiery talk in an outdoor facility, used for meditation and yoga, called the *dhyanamandir*. The three of us were arranged exactly as in my dream. His talk made a profound impression on me, even as I was enveloped in powerful déjà vu.

Many of us have experienced powerful prophetic dreams. Often, people ignore them, while others place extreme importance on them. The connection between indisputable parapsychological phenomena and the mystical process is very natural. Such phenomena often surface as we awaken the contemplative experience in our lives. Though these dreams are not the core of the spiritual journey, they do have a role to play. Often dreams provide essential guidance in or information about our journey. Biblical literature and many sacred texts of other religions are replete with examples of such guidance. Dreams are frequently a place of encounter with deceased loved ones who return to give us important information, and this information is usually beneficial to our own spiritual development.

In January 1986, my Uncle John and Uncle Teddy, his younger brother, first appeared to me in my dreams. I was very close to Uncle John, and he had died the preceding October. I had never dreamed of Uncle Teddy before that time or since. In this extraordinary visitation, both appeared, and Uncle John said simply, "We wanted you to know we are both in Heaven." It is difficult to express how much joy this dream, and its message, gave me. This dream was only the beginning, though. Over the years I've learned so much from Uncle John in dream consciousness. He always gives me vital information I suspected but didn't have.

Dreams can be important conduits of knowledge, insight, and practical wisdom. It is said that Emperor Constantine had a nocturnal vision that ultimately influenced him to become a Christian, a vivid dream in which he saw the cross in the sky with the words "Under this sign you will conquer." Shortly thereafter he embraced Christianity, and the Peace of Constantine commenced.

Another fascinating paranormal capacity is the gift of reading hearts. It is a gift that often accompanies the development of our contemplative selves. Reading hearts is a form of spontaneous discernment that I'd read about as a child in the lives of saints. I had the great privilege of witnessing this unusual gift in Uncle John's interactions with a number of people. He was able, without effort, instantly to know another's heart just by being in their presence. He discerned something essential about their nature, whether or not they were trustworthy, and he was never wrong. This ability sometimes disturbed me because he rarely approved of any of my friends, and yet he turned out to be right about them every time!

The contemplative journey introduces and develops this capacity in us. Uncle John had become a contemplative simply by consistently saying the rosary a few times a day. Reading hearts is really a highly activated form of intuition, and the mystical life greatly increases the range, depth, and accuracy of the intuitive faculty. Part of intuitive ability is clairvoyance, which literally happens daily for me. It is not uncommon, in my experience, to hear the phone ring and instantly know who it is or to know exactly what someone will say, before he or she utters a word. Sometimes I can feel where people are in a room without looking, while, at other times, I can know people's thoughts before they talk. Of course, I don't realize it in the moment of knowing, only after the information emerges.

When I graduated from college in 1971, I taught high school courses in comparative religion, anthropology, sociology, and English for the City of Hartford's adult education program. In the summer of 1976, the year before starting graduate studies at Fordham University, I was assigned a course in sociology. The course met four mornings a week for about ten weeks. There were around thirty students in the class, and one of them was a beautiful young Portuguese woman. Because she didn't have a baby-sitter, she'd always bring her seven-year-old son to class. Although I can't remember their names, I do remember their faces, because of a little daily ritual that went on during the entire session.

Every morning before class, as I was arranging my notes, the little boy would run up to the front of my desk, put his elbows up, and grin at me. I would respond to him with a little greeting, and he'd return to his desk near his mother in the back of the room, whereupon he'd color in his book for the rest of the period. I always looked forward to this daily interaction.

The course ended in August, and we all went our separate ways. Several years later, as I was walking down a street in Hartford, suddenly the boy's face came vividly to my mind. "I wonder what became of him and his mother," I thought to myself. I then imagined what it would be like if he were my son or brother, what I would want for him. This went on for five or ten minutes. I came to an intersection and decided to take a shortcut back to my home. As I turned up this street, I noticed three children walking ahead of me; one of them was taller than the other two. I decided to hurry past them, and as I did, the taller of the three looked at me. It was the boy from the class!

He looked at me with the same twinkle in his eye that he had shown years before, but there was something more — not just immediate recognition but a cosmic peek-a-boo the

Divine was playing with both of us. The boy was an instrument in communicating the mystery of transcendence — a purpose that went beyond him, though it also included him. This was the most impressive example of clairvoyance in my life, though, as I stated, smaller ones occur almost every day.

Divine protection, a further element of the spiritual journey, is a common feature in many lives. I have felt this presence all my life. So certain was I of God's care for me that, as a child, I would routinely cross streets without looking. Some might interpret this behavior as reckless, but it came from a place of trust and certitude. I knew I was safe because God was always looking after me. And this angelic protection has extended to my adult life. In early April 1987, I had just returned from India and had just visited some Franciscan hermits in Cummington, Massachusetts. It was about 10 P.M., and I was driving east on Route 2 near Amherst, when I noticed a car speeding toward me in the opposite direction. As soon as I noticed it and how close it was, I saw another car swinging out in front of the other to pass it. The driver had not seen me, and I knew an accident was inevitable.

Then something truly miraculous happened. As I sped along at fifty miles per hour, a mysterious force or presence gently but firmly pushed my hands off the steering mechanism and executed a maneuver that quickly removed me from harm's way a split second before impact. It removed my car only slightly off the road, and saved my life.

Although this was an amazing experience, it didn't actually surprise me at the time. I was, rather, inspired; it happened so naturally, like it was supposed to, that I didn't think much of it at the time. I believe, without a doubt, that some divine intervention occurred. This is the grace given to those who choose the spiritual path, regardless of their tradition.

the Four Essential Requirements

There are four essential requirements for successfully embracing a mystical path in the midst of the demands of family and work: surrender, humility, spiritual practice, and compassionate action. These elements are indispensable to being a mystic in the world, and they are part of a more comprehensive list of elements, with some overlap, that I have developed in *The Mystic Heart*.[12]

Each day, and in every moment of the day, surrendering to God, or to the greater purpose of our existence, is necessary. Relinquishing control over our lives to the Presence is essential if we really want to awaken and develop our capacities for the mystical, for intimacy with God. Along with this surrender, humility is indispensable, and indeed shows us our need to surrender. Humility is insight into ourselves — our motives, tendencies, gifts, and limitations. It protects us from self-deception and the egotism of the false self. Without humility it is impossible to maintain a spiritual life either in the world or in the cloister.

As I have stressed throughout this chapter, regular prayer or spiritual practice is the foundation and core activity of any mystic. It is a sine qua non of spiritual life in any tradition and must be pursued with diligence, perseverance, and faith. I have discussed several options, but of course you are free to adopt whatever practice you desire. It's useful to discern through trial and error what works best for you. There's a wonderful aphorism in the English mystical tradition: "Pray as you can, not as you can't!" In other words, find out what works for you, and leave the rest.

The final essential requirement is compassionate or loving action. This may be channeled through a commitment to some regular service program, or it may be spontaneous, as occasions arise that require a response from us. What's important is an integral experience of compassion: uniting the attitude or disposition of love and compassion with its fruits in acts of kindness and mercy. Remaining faithful to these four attitudes and activities will help to transform you into a mystic in the world.

Spiritual Practice for Parents

Needless to say, what I've outlined above, particularly those parts related to practice, are easier to pursue for a monk or contemplative with no family obligations. Everyone experiences pressures, but parents, especially those with infants and young children, face obligations and pressures that can make pursuing a spiritual life especially difficult. Below I offer some suggestions that should prove useful in creating and maintaining a foundation for a spiritual life for those in the active situation of family life.

It is vitally important to pursue inner experience even in the midst of parental obligations. It can be done, and with great success, but it takes determination, effort, and creativity. Both parents need a regular immersion in silence and solitude to restore themselves and to maintain their contact with the Divine. In finding regular periods for solitude and quiet, which are indispensable to deep prayer, it is enormously helpful to create a sacred space in your home; it can be a room, a corner, and even a closet!

A number of friends of mine, who are parents of young children, have taken this course. Two sets of these parents have opted for the inner closet in their bedroom, and this has afforded them an area of intense quiet and a place where they can find the aloneness before God so essential to the inner life. The closet has been tastefully decorated, and there is an altar on the floor, with a carpet covering the entire floor of the holy space. There are images of Christ, the Buddha, saints, and angels adorning the walls, and statues on the altar itself, with incense, holy water, candles, and a CD player for sacred music. The low lighting also helps to preserve the atmosphere of spirituality and commitment to prayer.

Usually when the members enter their little chapels, they will do some spiritual reading, recite a psalm of two, and then do an hour of meditation. They will do this twice a day, in the early morning before the children arise, and in the early evening or late afternoon before things get too busy again as the evening approaches with its family activities. Normally, they begin and end their periods of prayer in the sanctuary with some music conducive to their desire for prayer and quiet. It will not take children long to discover their parents' secret hiding place, and they will want to be part of this sanctuary. In the experience of my friends, the children naturally gravitate to the sanctuary when it's time for prayer. Often, they will sit in their father's lap when he's meditating. In this way, spiritual values and insights are being deeply absorbed. If children learn meditation, it gives them a huge advantage later in life. They will be much further along in their development when they reach the age at which their parents had begun to meditate or to take their spiritual lives seriously.

Another friend of mine is Keith, an American Baptist pastor with two small children. Years ago he designated his home office as his sacred space. No sooner had he implemented his decision and begun praying there than his son, Brendan, showed up, wanting to be part of what was going on. So Brendan began meditating with his dad daily. Now and then his younger sister, Kylie, would join them for prayer, especially for sitting meditation. Although his wife, Chris, doesn't join in at their sanctuary, she does do tai chi with him a few times a week. In the long run, it doesn't matter what your spiritual practice is as long as it helps you surrender to Ultimate Reality, maintain your intention and perspective, and promote love in the family and beyond. Wherever you are, you can create the rudiments of the spiritual life, working with what you have.

CHAPTER 3

Timeless
Mother

The Church As Matrix

In a powerful early Christian text traceable to the fourth century called *The Shepherd of Hermas* the Church is depicted as a wise old woman — cosmic, timeless, and otherworldly.[1] In this text, which was quite popular in its time, the Church is said to be the firstborn of creation.[2] She is wisdom personified, celestial, the giver of visions to Hermas, the protagonist receiving her messages. This eternal Church, brought into being before the creation of the universe, attempts to guide us through these visions. This is not the image of the Church as we have come to understand it, cultivated through the centuries by the various Christian institutions and theologians, but a view inspired by an eternal, even mystical understanding. The Church in the *Shepherd of Hermas* travels light, with little historical baggage. Through the lens of the Gospel, she sets her eyes simply on the priceless goal of the Kingdom of Heaven. This image of the Church celebrates her freedom to be what she is meant to be, untainted by the compromises the world often demands. It is paradoxically a view of the Church in her youth, before power's corrupting influence has set in, eating away at the integrity of this great institution.

For years I've reflected on this haunting image. The Church of *The Shepherd* is uncontaminated by the world and its inevitable political entanglements with nations and kingdoms. It is an image of ecclesial innocence and spiritual freedom — an image quickly lost with the Peace of Constantine in 312 A.D., when the Church joined with the Roman Empire. The Church of *The Shepherd* is an eternal church with a transhistorical mission to transcend worldly concerns and power politics. It belongs to a period of Christian idealism, when the freshness of the Gospel still inspired her. It is my belief that something of this innocence, informed by the ecumenical spirit of the interfaith movement, must be regained in our time. Regaining this innocence is an essential part of renewal and reform as she faces an unknown future, a future in which the Church can play an important role beyond Catholicism itself.

I call this mission of our interspiritual age the Church as matrix. This approach to the Church's self-understanding sets the stage for building an interreligious coalition, which can establish the groundwork for a universal civilization with a heart, a civilization of love. This realizes the precious dream of Pope Paul VI, who foresaw an age in which a new order of civilization would arise, inspired by the Gospel, and, I would add, draws on the best in all the great world religions, since a truly universal institution would require the particular genius of each tradition.

Before turning to a discussion of this vision, I would like to narrate my own early experience of the Church, how it shaped my understanding, and how that understanding shifted quite unexpectedly after I visited India. From there I will examine the problematic aspects of the Church, its historical roots in the Roman Empire, and the influence Machiavelli's book *The Prince* had on her thinking. This preoccupation, even obsession, with power has created a deep tension, indeed struggle, between the Gospel and the Roman Empire in the heart of the Church, vying for her loyalty.

THE CHURCH AS MOTHER

I have always thought of the Church as a mother. The image of the Church as a mother is an ancient, traditional association millions of Catholics make. But I have always regarded the Church as *my* mother, even though it has been difficult at times to maintain this affection. "It's easy to suffer for the Church, but is very difficult to suffer at the hands of the Church," the old saying goes. At times, I have suffered at the hands of the Church, particularly over my support of Tibet's nonviolent struggle.

When I say the Church is my mother, I have to add that she is the only mother I've ever really known. My own mother made a decision to favor her husband, my stepfather, who never accepted me and wanted to hide my existence from the rest of his family. Their marriage was based on the lie of my nonexistence. I tried in the early years to seek a relationship with them, my cousins, aunts, and uncles, but my mother's husband took it on himself to prevent me from having a relationship with anyone in the family. This blockage in my life has been a source of enormous suffering for me, though I've learned to accept it over time, moving on.

The Church was always a stable, nurturing presence in my formative years, providing a deep sense of security, comfort, and peace. Catholicism is a culture, not simply a religion.

Many subtleties of emotion, relationships, associations, and personalities compose the Catholic experience. Catholicism is also a sheltering atmosphere that protects the flock. The Church was a pervasive force of formation for me in my youth, one that I never questioned or challenged. I always accepted her teachings and guidance, with solid love and commitment. To this day, my love for the Church is profound and my commitment to her and her welfare is absolute. Yet this doesn't mean I can let pass instances that require criticism or challenge. Criticism isn't the same as disloyalty. I firmly believe that not speaking out when moral necessity warrants it does the Church a much greater disservice than challenging her does.

My youthful relationship to the Church was idyllic. I found enormous joy in being part of this exceptional community. The Latin mass, incense, hymns and Gregorian chant, the serene look of holiness in the images of the saints and their inspiring example, the nuns and priests, the special feast days, the fatherly presence of the pope — all these were powerful icons of my childhood and early adulthood. Catholicism wasn't simply my culture, it was my world, what I knew and cherished.

I had a special devotion to Mary, the Blessed Mother of God, as she is called in Catholic and Orthodox teaching. I saw the Church as an embodiment of Mary as much as of Christ, and so I identified Mary as mother, as my mother. Later in adulthood, at least by the time I was in graduate school in the late seventies, I began to realize that Mary was also a priestly figure for me and for others. A priest, through the celebration of the mass and the words of consecration, makes Jesus Christ present in the Eucharist, body, blood, soul, and divinity. So, in a very real sense, Mary was the first priest because she made Jesus present here in this world body, blood, soul, and divinity, as the formula goes, through her own body. Her acceptance of the invitation to bear the Son of God and his birth through her were the first eucharistic consecration.

Though the Church was changing and adapting to the twentieth century, my relationship with it in my twenties and thirties didn't change much. From 1962 to 1965 the Second Vatican Council introduced substantial, wide-reaching change to Catholicism. The vernacular mass was one of the first innovations, setting aside Latin, the official liturgical language of the Church, for special occasions. The tight discipline of the Catholic Church was loosened by the sense of change and renewal spreading all around the Christian community. Vatican II opened the Church to the world and to other spiritual traditions. It committed the Church to a direction that emphasized dialogue and mutual respect, with the promise of collaboration between and among the great world religions. More superficially, sisters retired their religious habits and donned secular attire. They started living in apartments rather than in convents. Many priests, mostly in Europe, began wearing ties instead of Roman collars and enjoyed greater personal freedom. Vatican II demonstrated that the Church was not immutable, that she could indeed alter her course and adapt to the times.

My identity as a Catholic was tied up with Rome; I was totally dependent on the structures of the faith. Theologically I was moderate to liberal, and although my mystical life was developing rapidly, my faith was firmly focused on the Church. My relationship to it had an obsessive quality, although I didn't see this at the time. I believe now that my attachment to the Church had a lot to do with the maternal function she played in my early life. My loyalty was blind and uncritical, my love silent before her abuses. I would never think of uttering a word of criticism, and I defended the Church even when her actions were questionable.

I was profoundly obedient to the Magisterium, the official teaching authority of the Church, and, of course, to the pope, he being at the head of the magisterial office. Even when I didn't fully agree with a teaching or a doctrine that needed updating or further development, I never took public issue with the Magisterium. Even in private I was guarded. I certainly would never write anything that might challenge Church authority or in any way embarrass her leaders, and more often than not I would defend Church doctrine, always giving the benefit of the doubt to leaders who followed policies that seemed out of step with the Gospel.

Then, in November 1986, I went to India, and everything changed. Gradually, India drew me more and more into my interior, or contemplative, nature. I began to let go of external structures. Bede Griffiths and I often talked of the Church, and he was also deeply committed to her, though he had no problem challenging her. He took her to task hundreds of times in his public discourses, articles, interviews, and letters to the editor of the *Tablet* in London, a Catholic weekly. The editor of the paper once told me that he had to tone down Bede's strongly worded letters before publishing them!

Over the course of my several visits to India in the late eighties, my attitude toward the Church changed slowly. But my realization of this change happened very suddenly while flying into Britain in March 1989 on my return from one of these long visits to the subcontinent. As the Air India flight was preparing to land at Heathrow, I thought to myself: "My God, how I've changed! I never saw it coming, but I've changed." This realization dug deep into my psyche, and with it came a profound sense of loneliness. I had lost my innocence about the Church and, like a child who realizes the fallibility of his or her idealized parent, I felt deep pain.

My youthful confidence in the Church had been shattered. My idealized, idyllic vision was gone, and the security, peace, and comfort of the past were replaced by uncertainty, anxiety, and discomfort. Although I still loved the Church, I began to see the institution for what it was — divine in origin, as my faith and the tradition hold, but composed of frail human beings with their own motives, at different stages of spiritual attainment. I realized very simply that individuals who come to positions of power in the Church, but who are not very enlightened, can do enormous damage. Usually, this damage is political and moral.

The Problems of the Church

As a Catholic Christian, in the openness and commitment of my faith, I have no problem with believing in the Church's divine origin and mission. Rather, I'm pointing here to defects in the moral, political, and prophetic dimensions of her operations in the world. Because people and the world are imperfect, there will always be some moral compromise in how the Church operates. But dedication to the Gospel should always rest at the heart of the Church's goals and actions. Unfortunately, this simply doesn't happen. The Gospel is too frequently compromised, especially for political goals. For example, when the pope, or other Vatican officials, soft-pedaled the moral struggle of the East Timorese, this was a failure to follow the Gospel, a failure with a political cause: unwillingness to offend the Indonesian government in order to gain concessions for the Church in the future. This is a typical pattern of the leadership of the Catholic Church. Because the institution of the Church operates in a political world, often at the favor of governments, it sometimes remains silent in the face of terrible oppressions and completely fails its prophetic purpose.

There are historical roots to these problems of power, moral limitations, and prophetic weakness. For 312 years after Christ, the Roman Empire mercilessly persecuted the Church. Many Church leaders were martyred. Then with the Peace of Constantine in 312 everything changed. The Church became respectable and then fully established. From the beginning of this intimate association between the Roman Empire and the Church, like an overwilling student, the Church learned the culture of power that had sustained the Empire for over three centuries. The Church went on to exercise this kind of power for 1,200 years. In a sense, the Roman Empire was the Church's stepmother, and the Church assimilated the nature, function, and the ways of power. Finally, when the Roman Empire collapsed two centuries later, the Church essentially became the empire. Later, under Christianity, the empire was resurrected as the Holy Roman Empire.

The Peace of Constantine, with its intertwining of Church and empire, vitiated the Church's witness to the Gospel. As popes and other Church leaders became increasingly involved in political struggles, a deeply corrupting influence entered and dominated the Church's functioning. In many ways, though the Church remains committed to the Gospel and its values, it is also, in a very real sense, a kind of ecclesial Roman Empire, with the pope as Caesar and the cardinals like the Senate of Rome. The Church is steeped in an ancient culture of power that has no sanction from Christ, which results from the Church's uncritical association with the powers of this world. It has become so much a part of Church culture as to be invisible to its leadership.

This culture of power was further refined during the Renaissance through contact with the practical political insights of *The Prince*, Machiavelli's treatise on government, a somewhat ruthless algebra of power and how to maintain it. Three basic influences thus inform the Church's self-understanding: the culture of power of the Roman Empire refashioned through the centuries of the Church's own needs, expectations, and vast political and diplomatic experience; Machiavelli's insights on the place of the ruler; and the timeless wisdom, values, and perspective of the Gospel, whose vision is totally counter to both the Roman Empire and Machiavelli.

The mixture of these influences has created a deep, divisive tension in the heart of Christianity. An ongoing struggle exists at the center of the Church, in Rome, between the demands of the Gospel and the demands of power and its maintenance — between the call of Christ and the temptation of Caesar. On the one hand the Church is solidly committed to the Gospel and is duty bound by her mandate from Christ to proclaim the truth of his Gospel on every occasion, which she does. On the other hand, the realpolitik of survival in this dangerous world can overcome the Church's higher function. There is a perpetual flip-flop between the demands of Caesar and the commands of Christ. It is an incredibly difficult path for the Church to negotiate, and in the past she has made terrible mistakes she has still not lived down. Jesus admonished the people of his time "to render under Caesar what is Caesar's, and to God what is God's."3 This balance has not been kept.

An essential part of the Gospel, and the Jewish milieu out of which it was formed, is the prophetic dimension that requires the Church to stand up to those who oppress the poor, who are a threat to peace, and who destroy creation through war and nearsighted economic policies. This prophetic dimension of Christianity, and especially of the Church, was frustrated during the reign of Pope Pius XII. This pope knew the responsibility of the Church and her leadership to confront the Nazi regime, but for his own reasons he chose to ignore this moral and prophetic challenge. He absented himself and the Church from taking an active role in squarely facing the Nazis and challenging their assumptions, ideology, and, most important, their heinous crimes against humanity — although he was instrumental in saving thousands of Jews.

Pope John Paul II, to his credit, has recognized that this policy of silence constituted a major blunder, one that might well take centuries to overcome. On one of his pastoral visits to Germany, he made a special point to honor German Catholics and other Christians who had openly opposed Hitler. The pope said that these Christians spoke for the Church in their opposition to the Nazis, even though the Church at the time was silent. The pope's extraordinary announcement establishes the precedent that ordinary Catholics — those with no ecclesial authority or office — can speak for the Church. In many situations the Church leadership may feel constrained and may retreat into silence. Others may then step in and give the necessary witness, whatever it may be.

A concrete example in our time is Tibet. The Catholic leadership in Rome feels unable, or unwilling, to raise its voice in criticism of the People's Republic of China or to express openly the Church's solidarity with the agonized Tibetan people. The reticence of the Church has nothing to do with the fact that most Tibetans are Buddhist, because there are also thousands of Tibetan Catholics who live in western China near the Tibetan border. Why the policy of silence? One can only say that the Church is motivated by politics and not by the Gospel. I will say more about the Tibetan cause in chapter 7.

If the Catholic Church is ever to know real reform, that is, if she is ever to come to terms with her history, her unique relationship with power, or her historical association with the Roman Empire, she has to be willing to admit that the Church herself, not only her leaders, has made serious mistakes and will continue to do so. The Church is a human institution as much as a divine one, and humans make mistakes. The Church makes mistakes, and this recognition is at least implied in the papal apologies at the dawn of the third millennium. In coming to terms with her past, the Church can also draw on her rich theological tradition and the various forms of lived spirituality present throughout Catholicism.

It is critically important to speak out in a prophetic instruction to Church leaders when they fall short in their policies and actions. Remaining silent only harms the Church. We know it is capable of bold leadership, as shown when John Paul II confronted communism in Poland and the Soviet bloc. The pope was a spiritual, intellectual, and moral catalyst to the awakening of the Polish nation in its historical manifestation of Solidarity. This was a genuine workers' movement, the kind that Marx claimed would typify the power of the masses and bring about revolution. What an historical irony — one that wasn't lost on the Soviets, who stood by and watched a classic awakening of the workers to the inhuman, oppressive system of communism. Eventually, this movement unraveled the entire communist system in Eastern Europe, and the pope provided a key element of leadership that made it a reality. This is what constitutes prophetic witness and leadership; this kind of leadership is what the Church and the world desperately need, particularly in these dangerous times — times made dangerous not simply by terrorism but also by the widening gap between the haves and the have-nots.

THE CHURCH AS MATRIX

We now face a new challenge and opportunity: the end of isolation all around the planet as previously remote cultures and societies open up to one another. The world's religions have been for millennia separate cultures, but now their boundaries are giving way as they find new relationships with other traditions and enter into conversation after centuries of mutual silence. Since the Second Vatican Council, along with extensive ecumenical and interfaith encounters in Europe, India, and America after World War II, the religions have been coming out of their self-imposed isolation, and through encounters with one another, have discovered common ground. This common ground is primarily a matter of those serious, practical issues we all face: injustice, abuse of human rights, economic exploitation and inequity, the pursuit of peace, spreading ecological responsibility, promoting educational and employment opportunities, and the desperate plight of refugees, women, and children in certain areas of the world. This loss of isolation has also created deep resentments in many conservative practitioners who cling to the closed primacy of their faith. We have recently seen this most dramatically in the violent expression of Islamic fundamentalism, or its most extreme political elements. But as the world's faiths continue to learn from one another, the small segments responsible for so much turmoil will slowly fade in their influence. They will wither, because, as Rumi said of such extremists in his time, "They are all fireworks, and no light; all husk, and no kernel!"

Through interfaith organizations like the Parliament of the World's Religions, the World Conference on Religion and Peace, the Temple of Understanding, the World Congress of Faiths, and the United Religions Organization, the followers of various religious traditions are discovering bonds of community. This profound and growing sense of community is the basis of the new relationship evolving between and among the religions themselves. It is the impetus for them to pursue collaboration on the above critical issues.

This experience of community among the traditions leads to an enthusiastic openness to the spirituality present in each one of them and an eagerness to explore spiritual life and practice across traditions, a unique phenomenon of our time that we can call *interspirituality*.[4] (Chapter 9 is devoted to this topic.) Interspirituality is not a new form of spirituality, or an overarching synthesis of what exists, but a willingness and determination to taste the depth of mystical life in other traditions. Interfaith encounter, interreligious dialogue, and the collaborations of the religions, whether through interfaith organizations or more directly in bilateral relationships, are becoming permanent features of a new global culture. Our knowledge of other religions and cultures is likewise increasing, opening the door to a universal understanding of religion, spirituality, and culture.

This is the scenario the Church faces at the dawn of the third millennium, a movement opening doors hitherto closed, forging relationships once forbidden, leading us to the horizon of a new universal civilization. In this context, the Church occupies the central place of matrix. As matrix, the Church would be a welcoming place for all the religions, an ecclesial vision of the nature of the Church *ad extra*, or the Church beyond herself and her ordinary flock. As matrix, the Church is a mother who offers her womb for the development of this new form of cultural and spiritual life to take shape. As matrix, the Church achieves a genuine universal spaciousness that allows diversity without doing violence to her self-understanding and mission.

The Church as matrix could become a progenitor of a civilization of love, as Pope Paul VI put it, a civilization motivated and governed by considerations of kindness, mercy, compassion, love, and nonviolence; a civilization in which political, economic, and military power have given way to the power of love, as we see it portrayed so irresistibly in the Gospel and as suggested by Lady Church in *The Shepherd of Hermas*. The wisdom of the Church is the wisdom of the Gospel, a living source of insight that emphasizes charity as the key not only to life but to the mystery of the Incarnation itself. The Gospel, like our Lord's parables, cannot be understood unless one first realizes and awakens to this depth of love or charity that Christ embodies and teaches us. It is not enough to possess a theological understanding; it has to transform our hearts and actions.

Although the Church certainly has a preeminent position regarding the means of salvation, and she possesses the fullness of those means by virtue of her intimate relationship with Christ, she also has a responsibility in our age to be a bridge for reconciling the human family. As matrix, the Church might strive to become a container for all humanity's noble aspirations. The Church could be a nurturer of interfaith encounter, interreligious dialogue, spirituality, interspirituality, work for justice, the promotion of peace, creating sacred culture, and teaching environmental responsibility and economic sustainability. With so many negative forces conspiring against these movements, the Church must embrace more of humanity's spiritual impulses. Just as the Church since Vatican II has opened to the Jewish people, the Spirit is inspiring her through the signs of the times to open to Hindus, Buddhists, Muslims, Sikhs, Jains, Taoists, Confucians, and indigenous peoples. As matrix, the Church would no longer see members of other traditions as outside her life. She would promote the study of these traditions, seek common ground and parallel insights, and encourage celebration of the major holy days of these traditions, like the Buddha's birthday, the fasting and prayer of Ramadan, and the various significant Hindu feast days.

As the Church becomes comfortable with her role as the matrix, a natural, organic development toward creating a permanent forum for the religions will take place, created by the religious traditions themselves, with the valuable guidance of the Church as representative of one of the great religions. The interfaith organizations can assist in shaping this forum, but the religions themselves must do it. For millennia, the religions have lived in mutual isolation, ignorance, and hostility, often causing terrible wars and persecution. This condition has weakened their enormous moral influence; divided, they were unable to challenge countless abuses of kingdoms and states, much less the abuses perpetrated in the name of the religions themselves. Once the great traditions have a permanent structure in which to communicate their concerns, insights, and methods, they will collectively become a potent force to check the often irresponsible actions of governments. This will add a significant element in the equation for global stability.

Above all, this organization must be based on equality and inclusiveness among the religions. A civilization based on love, on the depth of charity and compassion, is a real possibility, but it can bear fruit only if all religions are participants in this great enterprise, this huge process of human transformation. It requires the Church to accept her larger role and identity as matrix and to embrace this role and identity. It requires acceptance of a universal responsibility the Spirit has given her. The Church is now required to radiate Christ's radical love and not simply insist on his unique salvific role. It will also require the reform of capitalism, the promotion of ecological justice, and a commitment to the full development of all people, with special attention to their educational, economic, moral, and spiritual needs. It will teach the importance of nonviolence in all relationships. It will be a human order in which spirituality and interspirituality will be the highest pursuits. Economics and power will be the servants and resources of this new civilization rather than its masters.

A New Universalism

Vatican II, particularly with the promulgation of its decree *Nostra Aetate,* initiated a great age of dialogue, which has inspired the growth of the interfaith movement and interreligious learning. This dialogue has assumed three forms: the dialogue of the head, or academic and theological dimension; the dialogue of the heart, or the level of prayer, meditation, and other forms of spiritual practice, including liturgical celebration; and the dialogue of the hands, or the common collaboration on projects for justice, peace, the environment, and the other critical issues.

The development of dialogue between and among the religions has steadily raised expectations. Members of other traditions often view dialogue very differently from the Church does, as reflected in so many of her documents, especially *Redemptoris Missio* and the more recent *Dominus Iesus,* which together underscore dialogue and evangelization as twin values of the Church but also clearly regard dialogue as subordinate to evangelization. This subordinate notion is unacceptable to the other traditions, and the Church's insistence on it certainly complicates relationships with these traditions. The Church can maintain the twin values of evangelization and dialogue, but its language in speaking of other religions must reflect sensitivity and discipline.

There is a way out in the Christian insight on the Logos, or the eternal mind of the Divine as the Son, the second person of the Blessed Trinity. A more open approach to other traditions is consonant with the nature of the Logos, since it is infinite and inexhaustible in its manifestations. We must keep in mind that the Logos encompasses the whole universe and beyond. It includes the divine plan for the cosmos and the possibility of millions of other worlds and beings who are similarly called to intimacy with God. Just as we need to be open to the larger vision of the Logos and its activity in the universe, we should be open to its activity in other religions here on earth. The Church, at this juncture in history, lacks sufficient knowledge of the other traditions to pass judgment on them. It took the early Church fathers, the first Christian theologians, five centuries to sift through the wisdom of Greece and Rome, and the Church is only scratching the surface of the Asian traditions.

One of the great resources the Church would have in a matrix function is her own profound and vast contemplative tradition, her extraordinary mystical life. This tradition has served the Church well in the monastic sphere, in dialogue with Hindus, Buddhists, and Taoists. Just as monastics have been at the forefront of interreligious dialogue, they can be of enormous value to the Church in her role and identity as nurturer. The Cistercians, in the work of Thomas Keating, William Mennenger, and Basil Pennington, have been preparing the faithful through the spread of contemplative practice, which now reaches virtually every area of the Church. Thomas Keating's organization, Contemplative Outreach, and its dissemination of the method of centering prayer, with its integrative teaching on the spiritual life, presents the Church with a precious resource for this new age. Without compromise to her nature and mission, the Church will realize a new way of relating to other traditions, guided by the Spirit and the demands of our time. In this new challenge of assimilation the Church has a choice: to look back, taking refuge in the past, or to follow the lead of the Spirit into a future guided by love — the promise of the Gospel itself, and, I believe, the will of God.

The vision of the Church as matrix sets the stage for a renaissance of Catholicism that unites past and present with the future. All that the Church has been in her best moments, all that the present requires and the future asks, she can bring together, making a bridge for herself to the other traditions. Her theology, culture, spirituality, and social teaching can provide leadership in the interfaith movement, fulfilling a new identity that welcomes the diversity of the religions and their spiritualities. If the Church can embrace true diversity and pluralism represented by the world's great religions, then she can achieve a true *catholicism* that is more than geographic universalism. The challenge now is for the Church to become universal in that metaphysical sense.

The Church as matrix, without claiming a preeminent place for herself, could inspire the other religions and the various nations of the world, calling them to peace. If many responded, then all of them together could lead the world beyond war, terrorism, injustice, hunger, poverty, disease, and illiteracy. Together with other religions, the Church could build the new universal civilization with a *heart*.

Such a new universal society has always been a cherished hope of Christianity, and we find in the New Testament some of the operating principles of such a life-affirming community. The dream, the hope, the goal of a universal civilization with a compassionate, loving heart is inspired by the realization of what Jesus called the Kingdom of Heaven. It is already a reality, we are told in faith. In the Kingdom of Heaven everyone is equal; resources are shared, and people care for one another, working diligently to advance the well-being of everyone in the community, especially the most vulnerable. I am convinced the Church has the power to make this vision of the Kingdom a reality in our age. But to do so, it will have to shed some of its old rhetoric and actions. It will have to become far more inclusive theologically and less judgmental of other traditions. Perhaps this is too much to hope for, but if the Holy Spirit is at work in this vast institution, calling it to a new, expanded mission as matrix of future inclusion, such a miraculous change is possible and maybe even inevitable.

CHAPTER 4

Spiritual Friendship

A Jewel in the Midst of Life

All of us realize, I think, that friendship is one of the greatest, most fulfilling human joys. Each of us has, or should have, many friendships, and each of us can probably look back to a particularly important friendship in our childhood, a friendship that greatly nourished us in our need for companionship and acceptance, a friendship with someone with whom we could share our secrets and our dreams. I remember Uncle John often uttering these penetrating words like a hidden mantra: "Friendship is like a precious jewel, so hard to find and so easily lost." These words have made an indelible impression on me, and they came from one of my dearest friends in this life.

Ananda, the beloved disciple of the Buddha, once asked his teacher and friend about the place of friendship in the spiritual journey. "Master, is friendship half of the spiritual life?" he asked. The Enlightened One responded: "Nay, Ananda, friendship is the whole of the spiritual life." Jesus had his beloved friend, John; King David had Jonathan; St. Francis enjoyed the constant companionship of Brother Leo and his special friendship with St. Clare, who led the Poor Clares, the Second Order of St. Francis. Aristotle regarded friendship, along with contemplation, as one of the highest goals of ethics. Cicero, the Roman writer, showed in his treatise on the nature of friendship that the Romans valued it as much as the Greeks.[1] Plato discoursed on friendship in his dialogue the *Lysis*.[2] Monasticism in Europe in the twelfth century witnessed the explosion of spiritual friendship under the inspiration of the Cistercians, or Trappists, whose monastic observance, reflection, and contemplation favored the flowering of insight on the practice of spiritual friendship. These monks knew more about the nature and value of friendship in their day than we do in ours. And in India, a friend is cherished more than anything else. The reason is simple: While marriages on the subcontinent are arranged, friendships are chosen, like they are everywhere else, and so they are regarded as precious, lifelong commitments.

We may sometimes think of the spiritual life as being austere and lonely. But the truth is that building bonds between people is just as important as cultivating a practice and often the two go hand in hand.

THE NATURE OF FRIENDSHIP

Looking at my own life as a contemplative in the world, living at the crossroads of fundamental societal change, I want to explore here the vital nature and value of friendship as it functions in my experience. As a hermit monk in the Catholic tradition, I am naturally also a celibate. Neither marriage nor the joys of sexuality are options for me, given my commitment to the monastic ideal. This path is not a popular one, and I don't expect the worldly wise to understand it, but it affords its own joys and possibilities. For one thing, it has made it possible for me to appreciate how precious a gift friendship actually is.

Friendship meets a human need to be nourished and comforted by the companionship, laughter, and the wisdom of others. We benefit greatly when we are among people with whom we enjoy sharing time. Many less technologically developed societies around the world — as well as American college students! — have developed hanging out with friends into a high art form, and this capacity is a talent natural to the human family. We have an innate tendency to be social, to seek fellowship with those with whom we feel kinship and affection.

The nourishing, comforting, social qualities of friendship, qualities that define this extraordinary human relationship, are universal requirements of a healthy bond of affection in whatever corner of the planet we happen to find ourselves. In our frenetic existence, however, with its emphasis on individuality and absence of meaningful community, we are often left devoid of the deeper richness and texture friendship gives us. We are like refugees adrift in our mass culture, with its anonymity and lack of opportunities. We need friendships as much as we need community, and we require both, because they complete us in an essential way, contributing to our intellectual, moral, psychological, and spiritual maturity. Others complete us because we all share the same mysterious Self, or Spirit. In our families, communities, religious groups, clubs, associations, and friendships, we are ritualizing our need for wholeness, integration with the larger Self, our ultimate and permanent identity.

Friendship is thus a universal value present in every culture, at every time, in all the situations of human experience — in the most deplorable as well as the most sublime. The ubiquity of friendship eloquently verifies the subtler nature of our identity in our individual and collective participation in the one selfhood. We all feel the need to be immersed in its fruitful connection with our common self in the Spirit. And so, since it expresses and meets a universal need, it is also an important goal and must be one of the highest priorities in the lives of most individuals and cultures.

I have many friends. And I continually find our greatest joy comes when we share time with no other purpose than being together. Such joy characterizes all of my times with my Indian friends Russill and Asha Paul, and with my many friends with whom I practiced aikido for three and half years. In each of my friendships, laughter and joy predominate, which are among the greatest gifts we give one another. Russill, Asha, and I usually give a few retreats a year as a team. Normally the theme is a holistic experience of the Sacred, an essentially experiential approach to the Divine. It has become a tradition for us on the last night of these five-day retreats to perform skits. One of these skits the three of us have developed is, if I may say so, a hilarious portrayal of an Air India flight, where it is said all sentient beings are welcome, including cows, sheep, dogs, and cats. Although the skit has a basic structure, we also improvise, and our retreatants usually can't stop laughing, especially when they see Asha in the role of a flight attendant, Russill as a *dhoti*-clad Brahmin, wearing only a white cloth around his waist, and me as a stuffy Englishman.

Often it is similarity of interests that draws individuals together, and the common interest, whether a working goal, cause, or spiritual commitment, acts as the catalyst awakening relationships to this uniquely focused affection. A person who becomes our friend, which happens when we *really* begin to see one another, ceases to be the anonymous presence our society's indifference often dictates for most relationships and becomes someone we love and appreciate, in a bond growing more profound with the inevitable ripening of the years.

A common philosophy of life, similar politics, or social orientation, a work or cause shared — all these inspire people to form friendships. But deeper still, we seek friendship with those few who put us at ease and with whom we can really be ourselves. Most of all, we desire friends who create a safe space for us to be ourselves. Friends exhibit this depth of acceptance; they know who we really are and love us for it. This quality of acceptance, of cherishing, is one of the most treasured capacities of life.

Capacity for silliness is another serious measure of friendship. If we can be genuinely free enough to let our hair down together, to be carefree and vulnerable, then we know we have an authentic friendship. When I would visit my Franciscan friends, who were hermit monks in Massachusetts, we would spend nearly our entire visits laughing over church politics, larger society, or our own foibles. Our silliness was in service of poking fun at ourselves. Humor in friendship has no other end than the transcendence it introduces; it relaxes and comforts us. It is often the glue of affection; it attracts us to people, revealing to us their preciousness. Humor gives us access to one another's humanity, particularly in situations where seriousness prevails. It often breaks the proverbial ice, our usual uptight tension. It has a way of lightening things, of granting much needed perspective.

During my late teens, I experienced a profound fear of death, which stemmed from a confrontation with my own mortality and that of my Uncle John, with whom I lived. My uncle had adopted me when my mother married my stepfather, who didn't want me in the picture. I was suffering an inner dark night about death brought on by a crisis of faith. Uncle John knew I was going through some spiritual crisis related to death, and he tried to dissipate my fear by provoking me to laugh about it. Like a Tibetan elder training a young lama about the ubiquity of impermanence, he used repetition to make his point.

On dozens of occasions I would return home to a dark house except for a little lamp near the sofa. Uncle John would be laid out on the couch like a corpse, with his tongue sticking out. It was a pretty convincing sight, and the first and second time he did this he managed to frighten *me* almost to death! When I cautiously approached him and was about to take his pulse, he opened his eyes wide, grinned, and blurted out, "Scared you, didn't I?" *Terrified* me is more like it. After recovering from my momentary fright and irritation, I broke into a long fit of laughter with him. Over time, this little ritual, mocking death and the fears it arouses, cured me of my melancholy philosophical mood. With the help of my later mystical experiences, it propelled me into my enduring spiritual optimism. Poking fun at death had freed me from fear and eventually led me to a larger understanding of life.

It is undoubtedly a common commitment to faith, a similar view of the nature of existence, the purpose of life, and the destiny of persons that brings us together and solidifies countless relationships. I make this observation on the basis of what I've witnessed and on what is certainly true in my own case. It is definitely true of many of my friends; they are people with whom I have a lot in common, especially in a spiritual sense. Uncle John and I had our Catholicism as a foundation. The pursuit of knowledge and wisdom and the search for the Divine, or the spiritual journey, are powerful points of focus in friendship. Aristotle observed that lasting friendship must be predicated on a similarity of nature and not on attraction or utility. By the latter he is referring to those unstable friendships based on using one another.[3] Utility reduces the other to an object to manipulate and exploit for some hidden purpose. A friendship based on utility is founded on sand and simply not worthy of our attention.

Spiritual Friendship

An orientation to the Sacred makes a foundation on which lasting friendship can be built. Interest in, seeking of, and commitment to the Sacred, the Divine, in whatever form it may assume, provides the ultimate measure of growth in the lives of friends and within friendship itself. Orientation to the Divine, to God and the spiritual journey, opens up an eternal dimension to the friendship and permits a depth of sharing that doesn't happen at sports events, the theater, concerts, dances, or bars, where conversations tend to be limited to the popular culture of games, politics, or the movies. The spiritual journey, the mystical life, presents an ultimate context for the guidance of our friends and all our relationships to occur. It grants us a focus, a destiny, and a container for our personal spiritual evolution that is lacking in many other spheres of life, such as business, school, and recreation.

Having said all this, I have dozens of friendships with people who don't share my Catholic tradition, who often are not religious, though they are indeed spiritual, simply meaning they are open to the depth of meaning in their lives. This is certainly true of my countless Tibetan friends, who of course are all Buddhists. We don't have God in common — at least not in the conventional Christian sense — but we have the dimension of spirituality, the practice of compassion and love. These friendships are deep and lasting.

Christ's Example

Jesus clearly emphasized friendship with his disciples. The New Testament writers tell us of the great lengths he would go to stress a relationship with them based on love, or *agape,* as the Gospel calls it. This agapic love — friendship — is the key to grasping the message of Christ. In a very real sense, love is the message Jesus came into the world to teach; he came to impart this extraordinary knowledge and to transmit this capacity to us.

The Gospel proclaims, "God is love."[4] We might just as easily say, "God is friendship," and St. Bernard of Clairvaux actually makes this claim. Near the end of his life and ministry on earth, Jesus tells his followers: "I shall no longer call you servants. . . . I call you friends."[5] And as the Gospel of Matthew tells us, love, or charity, is the criterion for salvation.[6] Agapic love is a friendship that responds to everyone we meet, spreading the Kingdom of Heaven on earth through our openness to and care for others. Jesus invites us to extend our friendship not simply to those with whom we feel a certain affinity, but to all. He teaches us that no merit exists in loving those who love us and challenges us to love those we wouldn't ordinarily include.[7]

Jesus is very clear about the nature of this love, this intimate friendship offered to all by him and his followers. In the Last Supper narrative, something truly extraordinary happens. This pivotal story records the institution of the Eucharist, the sacrament of Holy Communion, but also something subtler about friendship and its relationship to Jesus' body and blood, which is Holy Communion itself. Speaking within the context of Jesus' coming passion and death, and telling how one of his disciples would betray him, the passage states: "The disciple whom Jesus loved was resting his head on the breast of Jesus."[8] Here, in the context of the Eucharistic last supper, is something totally new: the identification of divine friendship, or love, with the Eucharist itself. Jesus' friendship with John, and with his other disciples, is intimately united to the Eucharist itself, that is, to his body and blood. Friendship is seen in its supernatural light as a spiritual gift. The Eucharist is a gift and a means of friendship with God, and human friendship is transformed into spiritual friendship. It is agape that animates spiritual friendship. Although the human need for friendship is being satisfied, it is guided by a higher or supernatural ideal. Divine love defines the trajectory of spiritual friendship and makes it a beneficial influence on our human growth.

Spiritual friendship, based on agape, or selfless love, is universal. It is not limited to the personal preferences that often determine friendships. These preferences often lack the universal availability to others required of spiritual friendship. Christ understood friendship on a much higher level. He saw it as the bond connecting his community of followers, a bond characterized by his selfless and self-giving sacrifice of himself. He defines love and friendship in these terms: "Love one another as I have loved you. Greater love than this no man has, that he would lay down his life for his friends."[9] It is this spirit, in my understanding, that characterizes the nature of genuine friendship, and even more so, its spiritual form. As a Christian monk, it is this ideal that inspires me in all my friendships. It is certainly true that I frequently fall short of this ideal, but I do keep it before me, and I take it very seriously. Friendship represents a dimension of deep experience that, like a marriage, requires a steadfast commitment and a considerable amount of work. It is not easy, and it must never be taken for granted.

The Monastic Perspective

The long and rich experience of monasticism in the West has reflected on the nature and value of friendship for centuries.[10]

In fact, medieval monastics, both monks and nuns, had a much more profound understanding of friendship than we do in our age. Because they had more leisure time and more stability in their communities — the stability of spending one's life in one place — they enjoyed an intense experience of integration. Their stability and connection to a monastery were guaranteed by their vows, and their vows protected them from the fragmented life that so plagues contemporary civilization. The unhurried pace of monastic life presented ample opportunity for monks to explore friendship among themselves.

The period from the late eleventh and the entire twelfth centuries was really the golden age of monastic friendship. Figures like Anselm of Canterbury and Peter Damian in the eleventh century, and the great twelfth-century Cistercian saints and writers Aelred of Rivaux and Bernard of Clairvaux, wrote eloquently on spiritual friendship.[11] They were each masters of the art and had numerous close relationships both inside and outside the monastery. Loving and nourishing, the monastic community was like a greenhouse where intense cultivation of both the spiritual life and close human bonds took place.

Bernard conceived of the monastery as a "school of charity," a sacred dwelling where brothers live in harmony and mutual acceptance of one another. In this view, he improved on St. Benedict's appellation for the monastery: "a school for the Lord's service." One can say, though, that if rightly understood love, or charity, *is* the Lord's service. If the cloister is a school of charity, or love, it is then also a school of spiritual friendship. This insight into friendship as having a definitive spiritual nature takes the discussion deeper, and beyond where the Roman writer Cicero had fixed it. In his work *De Amicitia (On Friendship)*, Cicero defines friendship almost all inclusively: "complete identity of feeling about all things divine and human, as strengthened by mutual goodwill and affection."[12] One of these "divine things" is the area of philosophical speculation between friends and various types of spiritual practice, chief of which would be intense reflection, a meditative kind of thoughtfulness that we see, for example, in the philosopher emperor Marcus Aurelius.

The monastic tradition of Latin Christianity, in the articulation of both Gregory the Great, a Benedictine pope, and Isidore of Seville, prelate and scholar, places the emphasis on friendship's spiritual character, calling a friend in the monastic context a *custos animi,* or a guardian of one's soul.[13] *Custos animi* does not assume the casual relationship exhibited by most modern friendships; rather, it requires a commitment to the spiritual development of your friends, the active work for their happiness and salvation, an essential and comprehensive understanding of one another's inner state — really knowing our friends' hearts. It includes committed friendship's usual intense affective power, but it also serves our friends' ultimate well-being.

Spiritual friendship, whether it takes place in the cloister or in the world, carries with it the overarching implication of *custos animi,* a bond that should be understood in the light of eternity, not through the vagaries of time. The classical notions of friendship in Greece and Rome, the New Testament vision, and its continuation and development in monastic practice all contain this eternal perspective. Spiritual friendship is just as human as secular friendship, and the feelings are just as real; it is not abstract and off in the clouds, but very concrete and practical, affecting real people in the world.

The spiritual lives of Anselm, Bernard, and Aelred in the great Benedictine tradition were richly endowed with the blessings of highly cultivated spiritual friendships. Bernard actually brought a number of his friends into the monastery with him when he entered. Neither he nor Aelred nor the ensuing tradition of spiritual friendship among the Cistercians saw conversion as necessitating leaving friends behind in the world. They saw spiritual friendship as consonant with the goal of the search for God, of union with God, and the pursuit of holiness with loving companions in the context of the cloister and its emphasis on renunciation. Friendship was seen as a boon to the spiritual life, not as an obstacle.

Aelred experienced friendship as part of the journey to God.[14] Human and divine friendship become one as our love grows and reaches maturity. As it does, it approximates the culture of divine love in heaven. The monastery is a school of love and friendship, and in the practice of living out these bonds of selfless affection, we anticipate the mystical joys of heaven where all are united in loving God, and one another in him. In his book *Spiritual Friendship,* Aelred describes this experience of convergence:

> The day before yesterday, as I was walking the round of the cloister of the monastery, the brethren were sitting around forming as it were a most loving crown. In the midst, as it were, of the delights of paradise with the leaves, flowers and fruits of each single tree, I marveled. In multitude of brethren I found no one whom I did not love, and no one by whom I felt sure I was not loved. I was filled with such joy that it surpassed all the delights of this world.[15]

Friendship, in its spiritual dimension, should aid a person's relationship to God. In the monastic tradition, friendship only became an obstacle if it involved homosexual activity. There was a real fear of homosexuality in monastic communities, and the writers before, during, and after the twelfth century warned against the dangers of genital expression, although attraction and expressions of friendship were encouraged. Bernard and Aelred, in particular, seemed at home with an expressive affection between friends in the monastery and in society. After the Reformation, fear of homosexuality became exaggerated, and religious communities began to discourage what came to be called "particular friendships," exclusive bonds that didn't include the community. This taboo still exists in many Catholic religious orders. (Timothy Radcliff, formerly master general of the Dominican order, once remarked to me how one of his brothers in community observed: "It isn't particular friendship I worry about; it's particular enmities!")

But true friendship in a monastic context possessed an innocent quality that excluded sexuality.[16] If homoerotic impulses existed, as they surely must have, they were rarely expressed. A deeply ingrained cultural disapproval protected spiritual friendships from slipping into sexual liberties, and this protection was reinforced by the aspiration for union with God, holiness, and the life of perfection within the consecrated state of monks and nuns. All the monastic writers, and those who wisely guided their communities, understood the necessity for a monk to exercise discipline and self-control, especially in close friendships. It was this capacity for self-control that made the miracle of spiritual friendship possible.

As His Holiness the Dalai Lama points out in his discussion of self-discipline and sexuality, we often dismiss the notion of discipline because we think of it as being imposed by others rather than by ourselves for our own well-being. Sexuality has a tendency to become obsessive, with accompanying emotions that block out the possibility of other nuances between people, or between a person and the Divine. This may be why all the major religions restrict sexuality among those pursuing serious spiritual practice as well as provide guidelines for ethical sexual conduct.[17]

THE ELEMENTS OF SPIRITUAL FRIENDSHIP

A number of elements that characterize spiritual friendship in the monastic tradition are relevant to all spiritual friendships. They are (1) a common orientation in the pursuit of spirituality, (2) acting as mutual teachers and students, (3) a mutual sense of responsibility for and commitment to inner development, (4) sharing spiritual practice, (5) reflecting the other's condition and depth, (6) expressing Divine love, and (7) perceiving the Divine in each other.

Sharing a Spiritual Orientation

The first element of spiritual friendship is sharing a similar orientation to a life of meaning and depth, as we discussed above. Such friends are passionately interested in spirituality and the spiritual life; though they may not share the same path, they have each *chosen* a spiritual path. They are both committed to the mystical life. A friendship rooted in the spiritual dimension draws life from a living source of vitality, wisdom, virtue, and joy. It will also endure the vicissitudes of time. It becomes an integrating factor between and among friends, uniting them in a subtle culture of Spirit.

In the monastic milieu this element is easy to recognize, since the members of the community are bound together in their communal search for God. A common orientation doesn't have to mean the commitment to and practice of the same faith tradition, but it might mean sharing the values, attitudes, and activity of, say, contemplation or meditation. Even more, it often includes a similar commitment to compassion and love.

Acting as Teacher and Student

In monastic life, as in the religious communities of the Catholic and Orthodox churches, there is a place for mutual correction. This counsel is advised in the New Testament, especially in Paul. Correcting one another is an act of love when we have the other's good at heart. It arises out of a permanent commitment to our friend. Giving guidance and correction, advice and objective evaluation, particularly when asked for, is an important function of friendship. Of course, beyond the need for admonishment is the act of sharing mystical experiences and insights. Often these insights are related to prayer, the problem of temptation, the opportunities for compassion, the challenges of difficult situations. Spiritual friends alternate between being students of and teachers to each other. Over time, they learn much from each other's guidance and acknowledge that they have learned from each other.

Sharing Responsibility and Commitment

Friends united through a spiritual bond feel a deep sense of responsibility to each other, a mutual commitment to their moral evolution and spiritual development. Although they are concerned with this life, just like anyone else, they are also focused on the goal toward which we all strive, whether we know it or not, whether we embrace or reject it. That goal is salvation, or in other traditions, liberation through enlightenment. This commitment to and responsibility for our friends is an absolute; it is part of any friendship seen in the light of eternity.

Praying Together

Close friends whose friendship has its source in the Divine, whose friendship is nourished and protected by the commitment of *custos animi* — the willingness to commit to others as guardians of their souls — often share spiritual practice. It might be a nondiscursive, or thought-transcending, form of meditation, yoga, chanting, visualization, praying the rosary, celebrating the liturgy, meditative walking, or spiritual read-ing. Through shared practice, particularly in silence, two friends are drawn closer together in the mystery of the Divine Presence. To meditate in silence is very powerful; a subtle spir-itual communication occurs. It is especially significant when friends come from different traditions; it gives them an expe-rience of existential common ground. An old Irish Catholic saying is apt: "The family that prays together stays together." When I take a walk with one of my friends, when we meditate together, reflect on a book, or muse over theological issues, we are drawn closer in our common spiritual activity.

Reflecting Each Other

The act of mirroring each other's condition and depth happens automatically when two people trust each other and achieve a state of harmony. In close relationships, trust creates vulnerabil-ity, sensitivity, and openness. Each person becomes a mirror to the other. This quality of reflecting also often happens with a spiritual teacher. Indeed, the teacher reveals to you what is pres-ent in your heart, your previously invisible preoccupations. A spiritual companion can also do this. The same dynamic of mir-roring happens in a good marriage. At times it can be difficult to see so much of yourself, especially those parts of you that are painful to embrace, in the reflection of another, but it is a valu-able, indeed necessary, function of intimate relationships, bene-ficial to our psychological, moral, and spiritual maturation.

Expressing Divine Love

Spiritual friendship, in my experience, is nurtured and sustained in a common exposure to Divine Love. It arises continually from this source. Communion with the Divine maintains the depth of the friendship in the ineffable love of God. Like ordinary friendships — if any friendship can really be said to be "ordinary" — a growing bond of affection is a precious fruit ripening with age. Such an affection is quite natural and emerges spontaneously in time. Divine Love — the real common ground — circulates in and around friends, especially when they are peacefully in one another's company. When Divine Love is present, and the friends are responsive to it, they will slip into silence and contemplation, so awed will they be by its reality, power, and presence.

Perceiving the Divine

It is quite ordinary for spiritual friends to be able, naturally, spontaneously, and almost effortlessly, to discern the presence of the Divine in each other. When we are really awake, we cannot miss the presence of Divine Reality; it is always calling us. The mystical process makes us more sensitive and receptive to it. It also increases our capacity to be aware, to know the Divine Presence in another's will, that is, to know that the other has surrendered to God or is continuing the ongoing work of surrendering. Yet this Presence has other subtle modes of expressing itself, and one significant way is through us, notably when we genuinely give ourselves to God. If one is living a holy life, with a genuine awareness of the Divine, that person usually has the ability to discern the Presence in others.

THE CAPACITY FOR FRIENDSHIP

I often say that contemplatives have a gift for friendship. Certainly many prominent figures in the monastic tradition have shown it. Their openness to God in turn opens their hearts to others, and their natural generosity combines with their desire to share, liberating their capacity to give themselves in attention, meaningful conversation, and acts of kindness.

These qualities were present in the friendship between St.

Francis and Brother Leo, and between St. Clare and Francis. They were part of the rich friendships in the monastic world of the twelfth century and beyond. The Spanish mystics of the sixteenth century, St. Teresa of Avila and St. John of the Cross, displayed these characteristics in their extraordinary friendship. Spiritual friendship, ultimately characterized by the spirit of *custos animi*, requires considerable growth in love and psychological maturity. Genuine spiritual friendship is not possible if one's behavior is based on selfishness. Nor can the friendship be fruitful if it is too one-sided, a common condition in ordinary friendships. It is only through the transforming power of Divine Love that we become fully integrated psychologically; then the conscious, unconscious, and superconscious work together, animated by this love.

My capacity for friendship has grown over the years. As a child I was very shy. Though I became more outgoing as only a teenager, I really came into my own as a friend to others in early adulthood, when I knew myself better and understood my need for friends and my desire to be available to others in the same way. Over the years, as my spiritual life has evolved, my talent for friendship has grown as well. I've learned much from my increasing number of friends, especially about the value of friendship. I tend to put great effort into being a friend to my closest companions. I am loyal; I try to listen carefully to them; and I like to spend time with them. But I place special emphasis on simply creating time to hang out and bask in my friends' company.

With the demands on my time — like everyone's increasing demands — it's not easy. I realize that as a spiritual friend I'm far from the ideal, but I push forward in the right direction, and I continually try to make progress. I feel a sense of responsibility and commitment, but also a respect for my friends' freedom. I try to be profoundly aware of all of my friends. I realize all my friendships are, in some sense, eternal, and that I must always try to act from that realization.

Tools of Spiritual Friendship

The skills of friendship are many: other-centeredness, honesty, availability, willingness to listen, sensitivity, generosity with time, helpfulness, the capacity to be completely yourself, and the willingness to place friendship at the service of the community. These capacities, like so many threads, weave friendship into a beautiful fabric, precious to those so blessed. All these skills work together and are interdependent. To take one out is to unravel the whole fabric.

All friendship requires other-centeredness. A friend does not focus on self. This other-centeredness must be based on honesty and a mutual caring. A deep trust must exist between friends that they are telling the truth. Honesty also extends to emotions. True friends do not suppress their feelings for each other, but often express them, when appropriate, and they are always willing to challenge each other when either perceives that something's wrong. In this way, friends are vehicles for each other's growth.

To develop true friendship, we have to actually *be* a friend to others. We cannot simply desire friendship; we must live it. A true friend is always available; availability is a sign of a friendship's authenticity. Friendship demands a willingness to listen, and this quality is closely aligned with availability; it is a listening with the intensity of the heart, not just to words, but to feelings as well. Such a listening is a form of sensitivity, allowing ourselves to feel and care, to be aware beyond our self-interest. This sensitivity is awareness itself, which is always growing in its capacity to understand and respond.

Friendship needs time, not simply in terms of its development, but in terms of its existential reality. Friends simply have to commit to spend time together. Then time itself, as the friendship matures, allows it to deepen and realization reveals to us how much of a treasure it actually is for us. A true friend is always willing to help and never counts the cost of time or resources. This skill for generosity is often tested, as are all the other skills. A spiritual friendship is predicated on being a soul friend, a companion along the inner way, relating the relationship to its center in the mystical life. Most of all, friendship means being totally yourself with your friend, and this requires relaxation, being at home with friends, not somewhere else, and not tense. When I'm with my friends, we are relaxed and we laugh with vigor and gusto. Spontaneity is expressed in banter, teasing, and endless humor.

Finally, spiritual friendship serves the community; it has value not only for those involved in it but also for the wider circle of humanity that benefits from the fruits of the friendship. Everything we do or accomplish of a moral, psychological, and spiritual nature has an impact on others. We are here not simply for ourselves; we are part of a much larger fabric of being and life. This beneficial relationship to community is another expression of the other-centeredness so essential in spiritual friendships.

Each skill is a tangible manifestation of love, and each requires its guidance. All these skills work together in weaving that majestic tapestry of divine friendship enfleshed in human beings here and now. No life is complete without this dimension of human association bridging the gap between earth and heaven. As a monk living in the world, I have found it to be my greatest human support.

CHAPTER 5

Keeping Our World in Order

The Preciousness of Time, the Sacredness of Work, and the Use of Money

James Yellowbank, a Native American friend of mine, is fond of an aphorism that underlies much of his tradition's wisdom: "The task of life is to keep your world in order." As a contemplative in the world, I have found that so much depends on this task. Monastics strive to be masters of keeping their world in order and harmony, balancing a schedule to permit sufficient time for prayer, work, study, and recreation. Maintaining balance in their world requires the nourishment of their souls, bodies, and minds, all in the context of a community that supports them in their common goals.

It is much the same for a contemplative hermit outside a monastery's community. Here I want to reflect on three very practical, yet central, aspects of my life in the world. They have a direct bearing on our aspirations for spiritual development, with or without family responsibilities, job commitments, and other demands on our time. These are ongoing struggles in all our lives, yet we often divorce them from our consideration of spiritual matters. In this chapter I want to explore the spiritual dimensions of time, work, and money.

The Preciousness of Time

Time encompasses the whole of any person's existence, the span of every lifetime. We cannot escape it; each of us faces the same passing of hours, days, and years. The human condition is always measured by its passage. Keeping time's ubiquity in mind, the difference between a monastic, or sacred, view of time and a secular one is really the difference between time and eternity.

With a sacred understanding, we view all time as contained by eternity, and therefore, we see time as having eternal significance. Paradoxically, we should think, feel, and act in the light of eternity, while at the same time being responsible and present in each moment. I am not trying to devalue time in a preference for eternity, nor am I devaluing the world or nature, the stage on which temporal events happen. Far from it! The nature of time is surrounded by, integrated in, and defined by eternity, which is the Now of all time, all events. In every age and epoch, the one eternal Now contains everything, and every moment of time is simultaneous to this one all-embracing, eternal moment. Eternity is the true essence and measure of time's ultimate value; it is its actual reality.

We experience time as completely and concretely real, yet time is subjective. Kant even called time a subjective intuition, meaning directly experienced along with space. Experience is impossible unless it is located in space and time. They are both subjective intuitions, conditions that allow our world to exist for us.[1] Time and space depend on our conscious awareness, and they adjust to our inner states, especially our psychological, intellectual, and mystical states. In a sense, they are our perceptual constructs.

A Thought Experiment

Let's try a thought experiment to help make Kant's insight more concrete. This experiment requires concentrated reflection, and it will help orient us toward the meaning of time, this elusive mystery that has baffled so many great minds throughout history, from St. Augustine to Martin Heidegger. Ask yourself these questions: Where is the yesterday that was once today? Where is this moment tomorrow? And where is tomorrow today?

Each moment of experience comes and goes, whether it is pleasant, unpleasant, difficult, or easy. Our intense loves, ecstatic, mystical perceptions, our experiences of incomparable natural beauty, all the mundane, everyday events of our lives are all here and then gone, receding into memory. But what of time itself, each moment it presents to us? Where does it go? What remains? Is it memory? Does time reside in memory when we look back? Memory is itself a thread of identity, for without it, we cannot recognize any past experience as actually belonging to us. And what of future moments? Where do they dwell? Consider what is present in each moment of time for you, that is, in your own experiences. It is not simply an external world or the objects behind all the events that pass so quickly in your everyday life. Of course, memory is useless when we look to the future, so it cannot be the basis of time. What is the constant in every event, every moment, every experience we perceive? The answer is very simple: consciousness!

Time and Consciousness

Time is maintained in and through consciousness, our awareness in each moment. In our thought experiment, let us see time as a line extended in space, with moments of experience as points along this cosmic line. What all these moments have in common is consciousness itself. It allows them to be through someone or something's awareness of them. When we look back at our life — our childhood, adolescence, and adulthood — it becomes clear that consciousness is what holds our whole life together. We thus realize the profound subjectivity of time.

We all find that time accelerates as we grow older. In childhood, time moves slowly, probably because we are so much more immersed in the present moment. Time also moves very slowly when we are bored, watching the clock, wishing time away. When I practiced aikido, though I loved this martial art and my many friends with whom I practiced, I found the falling difficult. Unfortunately, it's essential to the practice, so during class I often found myself looking up at the clock every five minutes, feeling the hour stretch interminably. Obviously my discomfort colored my perception.

We've also all experienced what can be called a temporal dilation, when a few seconds or a few minutes seem like hours. Mystical experiences or moments of extreme crisis often involve these dilations, in which brief moments seem extended. This occurs when looking within, in the mystical state of consciousness, or during deep meditation, where we transcend the so-called objective duration of the outside world. Our subjective time stands still or slows down. Inner awareness is the key to this dilation. Inner subjective time, or our perception of time, has a transcendent capacity to stretch or shrink itself.

Making Time for Our Spiritual Path

With this innate transcendental capacity comes the responsibility to use time wisely — not to squander it on all the wasteful pursuits and activities we are accustomed to in the West. Time has precious value — whether subjective or objective — because of its scarcity. We have only so much of it in this life, yet we spend most of our days feeling as if life will last forever. I know I have wasted a lot of time! A spiritual understanding of time such as monasteries strive for — an understanding that measures a mystic in the world — is founded on the realization that all time is a function of the eternal. Everything is seen in the light of eternity. Paradoxically, what this understanding means is that with every experience of time and every event of our life, we have to take into account its place in the larger framework of a reality that doesn't pass away. And it is this insight that makes time so precious. A spiritually alive and mature human being enjoys the present moment, and everything that makes life so fascinating and exciting. He or she also knows the graciousness of unprogrammed time.

To seriously follow the spiritual journey, particularly amid our world's busyness, one must learn to guard the preciousness of time by savoring the beauty of our periods for prayer or meditation, reflection, reading, work, study, and relaxation. Awareness of time's value and a commitment to live one's spiritual journey in this consciousness is a test of the maturity of a person's spirituality. Only by guarding one's time against the onslaught of distraction can we advance in our commitment to the mystical dimension of our existence. Only when we regard time's precious relationship to our inner life, only if we understand its necessity for spiritual growth, can we begin to use time more wisely.

Again, this wise insight is an essential part of monastic wisdom. Those of us who are monks in the world, mystics living on the edge of a society, must strive to be examples of a saner lifestyle that knows the purpose of time in relationship to our ultimate goal of spiritual transformation. No matter how busy or demanding our lives are, if we choose to live the spiritual life, we can take a stand by allowing structured time for prayer, meditation, spiritual reading, and reflection. We are very good at *doing* so many things; we need to develop our capacity for *being*, for being present to the integrity of each moment and the power that the right use of time has to achieve those significant breakthroughs in our journey to the Divine.

When I consider how much time is wasted in our culture, when I think of all the time I myself have wasted, I realize the importance of emphasizing the point that time is really a carrier and container of our spiritual aspirations — all our dreams, desires, and goals. We need constantly and urgently to remind ourselves of time's preciousness. Of course, doing so runs counter to the culture we are steeped in, a society in love with speed, excitement, the new, the different, the fashionable. To understand the nature and value of time, to grasp and live in its precious atmosphere is actually a *contemplative* quality. Our culture has a secular notion of time. Time for most Western societies is a profane reality, while the sacred aspect is parceled out to worship on the Sabbath. We have allowed the deeper view of time, conveyed to us in our sacred traditions over the millennia, to slip away into the sea of profane time where everything becomes colored by the ordinary, the mundane.

To regain the primordial, pristine vision of duration, of the integrity of the moment with all its possibility for depth, perception, and relationship with the Divine, we need to measure it in our daily lives, like monastics do, by providing places in our schedules for contemplation, meditation, or prayer — or perhaps a meditative walk, some yoga, chanting, singing, sacred dance, spiritual reading and reflective pondering of what we read, and time to examine our conscience each night. By creating a schedule that honors our spiritual life, we are consecrating time to a higher purpose, the purpose it has always had, the purpose for which it was intended. The whole sacral purpose of time is to promote our growth and the ultimate welfare of all sentient beings. Time is the golden string of inner realization.

Through our attempts to live a spiritual life in the world by following our individual *horarium,* the monastic word for a schedule that permits us to explore our inner experience daily, we are reclaiming the true value of the temporal. And we are doing this for everyone, as do monastics, gurus, spiritual masters, sages, and saints.

In the wonderful documentary *Baraka,* director Ron Fricke films spectacular scenes from life and nature in twenty-nine countries on six continents — without a single spoken word.[2] *Baraka* is a Sufi word that means blessing, and the film, premiered at the Parliament of the World's Religions in 1993, is a mystical and poetic tour of the planet, a kind of transcendental state of the world. One cogent scene in this powerful and inspiring film shows people in Tokyo amid the hustle and bustle of going to work, to school, and home. But in the middle of all this frantic coming and going walks an extraordinary monk completely absorbed in the Now of his extremely slow meditation walk. He rings a bell and holds a begging bowl. He never looks left or right, but concentrates on meditation through his simple act of walking with awareness. This monk, in his own way, is reclaiming the precious spiritual reality of time. He is restoring its original quality, its timeless nature. We must do the same in our spiritual lives by giving time its proper place as the container and guardian of our mystical journey.

THE SACREDNESS OF WORK

Just as time orders and measures our life's activities, work orders our life's purpose and the resources we require. Our ontains an innate dignity when it is truly connected to *us* — when our creativity finds concrete expression in what we do, how we shape our environment, in the fruits of our efforts. Work is holy, sacred, and uplifting when it springs from who we are, when it bears a relationship to our unfolding journey. For work to be sacred, it must be connected to our spiritual realization. Our work has to represent our passion, our desire to contribute to our culture, especially to the development of others. By passion I mean the talents we have to share with others, the talents that shape our destiny and allow us to be of real service to others in our community.[3]

It is this balance that enhances the sacredness of work, because it allows our talents, our innate creative passions to express themselves positively for the benefit of others. The root of this balance is purity of intention: the state of the heart itself, that point within the depths of our subjectivity from where motivation springs. It is a noble aspiration to contribute to the improvement of the world in some meaningful way. It's simply not enough to be successful economically; our lives have to possess meaning and value in relation to our community.

In the monastic world, work plays a central role, since monks and nuns are meant to be self-sufficient, and their work is always, or nearly always, meaningful. It has the quality of right livelihood that Buddhists recommend. Christian monastics operate large farms; bake bread and pastries; make candy, jams, and exquisite vestments. All these activities require regular, creative effort — the real key to meaningful work. As long as what we do is good for the world, the important thing is that we do it well, with a creative and disciplined mind always returning to the larger good. Labor is a disciplined activity, and while engaged in it, monks and nuns strive to be conscious of their purpose: union with God. Their work sustains them; it makes possible their prayer life, their recollected state of contemplation, and the relentless pursuit of mystical union with the Divine.

As a hermit monk and contemplative living in the city, I strive to be equally self-sufficient in solidarity with my brothers and sisters in the world and in the cloister. I identify with all those earning a living. I face the same realities they face: expectations from our boss and co-workers, deadlines to meet, the social and political dynamics of work, the stress of commuting to and from work each day, the noise and confusion of the workaday world. In handling these realities I try to apply the fruits of my spiritual life, to introduce that peace arising from contemplation to all my activities.

I am very fortunate to have variety in my work. I am an adjunct professor in Chicago's DePaul University, Columbia College, and the Catholic Theological Union, where I teach comparative religion, ethics, and spirituality. Throughout the year I also give retreats. These retreats always have a holistic theme of integrating body, mind, and spirit; East and West; and meditation, yoga, music, art, and nutrition. In addition to teaching, I lecture at various places around the country. And I give one-on-one spiritual direction to a few people. I am also committed to the ongoing activity of interreligious dialogue, which I pursue in the context of the Parliament of the World's Religions, conferences, and personal arrangements. One of my favorite forms comes in public discussion with members of other faiths, such as the informal Buddhist-Christian dialogue Sogyal Rinpoche and I conducted at a conference of the Association for Global New Thought. Finally, my work also involves writing. This variety is wonderfully enriching, and I feel very fortunate to engage with so many people on the matters about which I am passionate.

Teaching is my primary passion, however. It is where I get my greatest fulfillment, and I always strive to make this work sacred, which requires a specific approach. First, it is fundamental, I believe, not to consider myself above my students. To do so creates a false dichotomy that detracts from the learning experience and the joy it can give both students and teachers. Spirituality always strives to promote the conditions for genuine community: equality, availability, openness, freedom of inquiry, dialogue, teamwork, a sense of the sacredness of all our relationships. I regard my students and colleagues as sacred, because they are.

The first thing I try to do is to put my students' minds at ease. Some are always initially worried about grades and how a new professor will view them. I tell them not to worry about their final grade. To be obsessed with and motivated by getting a high grade is really working for a false goal, the wage of the grade itself, and it places an obstacle in their way to truly learning. So I reassure them about the need to relax and enjoy the course and their fellow students. This approach, for me, concretely embodies compassion in my work and is an example of how one's spirituality finds a place in the everyday situations of life. Ultimately, all our activities are opportunities for growth, including the important function of work.

For the mystic in the world, within our commitment to earning a living, our task is always the same: to bring light to an activity and dimension of our ordinary experience that is often darkened by the uncaring coldness of capitalism. I live from the center of a mystical realization, a depth of awareness that illuminates life, offering the key to the mystery we are all immersed in. Consistency in each moment and experience is the goal, not the fragmented existence that oppresses our culture. Consistency through the discipline of a spiritual life and the application to my work and the people I meet of the precious awareness that comes from that life — this is my ultimate goal in career and work.

There is an eloquent and potent simplicity in this consistency, but it is for me a grace, a gift the Divine grants to all those who seek relationship with it. It is the gift of perspective, a vision of wholeness that integrates all aspects of life in the one thing necessary: relationship with the Source. Each one of us is called, even destined, to gain this understanding, a right view that orders all our relationships and every aspect of our life. It is a single-mindedness that guides us into a steadiness of action, a habit of spiritual life that colors our work, our family, our friendships, and all our interests. This single-mindedness is the thread that runs through all aspects of our life.

Perspective, the gift of vision, gives us a powerful determination to live out of the center of our realization. Determination is the key. I remember how this insight was transmitted to me by His Holiness the Dalai Lama. I was leaving his home after a long conversation during my first visit to him in Dharamsala in 1989. As I turned to say a last good-bye, he raised his hand, pointed to me, and said with a smile: "You must increase your determination!" He had rightly discerned my need to become more single-minded in my practice, to develop and maintain the requisite perspective in every situation. I continue to strive toward that goal.

Spirituality in the Workplace

We each have to find this persistent determination ourselves. But how can we extend our daily spiritual practice — and the awareness it generates — to the workplace? Below I suggest some practices for promoting and maintaining spiritual or contemplative awareness at work. These practices — spiritual reading, meditation, contemplative walking, discussion groups, and some form of compassionate service — are meant to stimulate and nourish this awareness.

Reading. Many people read during their lunch hour. This activity continues the old monastic practice of table reading during the noon and evening meals. At work, people can take a book conducive to their mystical aspirations, and with concentrated reading, nourish their inner lives. They can take time to eat and then retire to a corner or a park bench, or sit under a tree, and read, absorbing deeply. Because spiritual reading feeds our inner awareness, it is a critical function of contemplative experience. As I discussed in chapter 2, in monastic life, and the Catholic tradition more broadly, spiritual reading is called *lectio divina.* It has a direct relationship to contemplation and is a method for cultivating its emergence and growth. *Lectio divina* is a practice that spontaneously flowers into mystical contemplation, in which the person is united to God in love and divine wisdom.

Meditation. Meditation is another spiritual practice that can find a place at the office, in some special room set aside for this purpose or anywhere you feel comfortable. Just as you may meditate regularly at home twice a day, you can also find time from your lunch break to sit quietly in the pursuit of greater awareness. People can meditate individually or with others at the office. Indeed, the practice of contemplative group meditation at work can also become an example for others, even executives and upper management.

Just as spiritual practice has lasting benefits for individuals, it can also radically change corporate capitalism, a system that tends to dehumanize and exploit if not kept in check by human values. Of course, many corporate executives exhibit real integrity and depth in their business relationships, but capitalism itself needs to develop compassion as at least one of its intentions.

Meditation, as a daily practice of awareness, becomes a vital tool to transform awareness in the corporate world, just as it does in individual lives and communities. It creates a corps of people who share a transformative activity in the heart of the business world, inviting that world to change, to grow in ethical understanding and compassion. Although a group of meditators in a corporate setting may seem insignificant, small developments like these often bring about great cultural change. Group meditation could eventually spark a spiritual revolution! Consider what would happen to capitalism if every corporate executive meditated twice a day. In time, the whole corporate structure would face the onset of a progressive awareness, calling people to inner transformation and compassionate intentionality.

Contemplative walking and other mindful exercises. For those who would like to engage in a more active form of spiritual practice during their break or lunch hour, a contemplative walk, tai chi, or yoga can do wonders. Contemplative walking, as I stated earlier, is different from the Buddhist practice of walking meditation, a deliberately slow and mindful practice. Contemplative walking, while mindful, can be done at any pace. One remains mindful of nature, consciously connecting with it, becoming aware of its presence, beauty, and values. I usually take a contemplative walk every day, and my best ones last an hour or so, but by keeping the walk to twenty minutes or so, you can fit it into a lunch break. I find great satisfaction and delight in walking by Chicago's Lake Michigan and watching the moods of the lake change. For me, as it was for Thoreau, walking is a form of prayer, of contact with the Divine.

Discussion groups. Another possibility for spiritual practice at the workplace is holding a discussion group. Group members can take turns leading the group and suggesting books, articles, videos, and music the members might explore together. These explorations can take root in the members' personal spiritual experience, but some of the most mind-expanding discussions can come from exploring other faiths and traditions. Just as spiritual reading should nourish the inner life, these discussions should also. A discussion group should not become a forum to vent and complain or to talk about work. There are plenty of other opportunities for that. This group exists to allow insights helpful to everyone's development to emerge.

Compassionate service. Compassionate service is the proof of spirituality, the evidence of genuineness and maturity. Those who are seriously committed to their spiritual life should be given opportunities to reach out to others who are less fortunate. You can find ongoing projects of service involving some of your co-workers and even family members. Although group projects are probably best, individual efforts can be just as valuable. Reaching out can be a spontaneous action, like responding to a homeless man or woman on the street. It can take the form of tutoring an inner-city child, visiting elderly shut-ins or the sick in hospitals, teaching meditation to prisoners, volunteering in a soup kitchen, listening to a troubled youth through a boys and girls program, working pro bono during your lunch break. The possibilities are endless. Although the rewards aren't immediately obvious, all these activities create just as much good for you as for those you help.

These are only five suggestions for bringing spirituality into the workplace — for ultimately increasing the depth and awareness of our inner lives. There are many other possibilities. It's

up to each person or group to come up with approac
enhance the workplace with programs that cultivate an
tain their spiritual lives. Companies can establish a committee
to investigate ways to develop programs and resources to guide
the process of allowing spirituality to flower in the workplace.

THE USE OF MONEY

We all must focus some attention on money, whether we like
it or not. But my interest in the use of money surpasses typical economic concerns. In the monastery, all property is held
in common by the community. Money is included as part of
the common trust, owned by the monastery and its members.
This arrangement helps to prevent money, property, and possessions from being seen as ends in themselves. Materialism is
perhaps the deepest pit our society has fallen into. One of the
most serious obstacles to building a universal civilization
with a heart — a compassionate world structure of government, commerce, and culture — is the attitude that the goods
of this world are ends in themselves and that in their pursuit
people are essentially expendable. Only injustice, economic
oppression, and exploitation can result from such a heartless
capitalism, or from such an immature understanding of capitalism. This is what prevents the world from making any real
progress.

Becoming a spiritually aware person means not accepting
this grasping attitude; it means realizing that it is based on
ignorance of what will produce the ultimate good for the
world. The purpose of life has nothing to do with generating
capital or being a cog in the wheel of a global economic system.
It is not about using others as a means to produce wealth. It is
rather about awareness, about love and compassion, and about
union with the Divine. It is about consciousness and the quality

of our awareness. If these values were firmly in place in our lives, then globalization with a heart and capitalism with a conscience would inevitably follow.

As a monk in the world, I have only a little money, compared to countless others in our society. Yet the money I earn from teaching, lecturing, and giving retreats is sufficient, because my needs are modest. I live in a small apartment with a reasonable rent. I don't own a car, and so I use public transportation. Although I do have medical insurance, which I believe is a necessity, I do not have luxuries that others take for granted. Again, I live very simply.

At the same time, I am committed to sharing some of the money I earn. I prefer to use what is left over after my expenses for homeless people I know. For me sharing what I have is a spontaneous process. I don't have this process organized in a systematic way. I will elaborate more on my relationship with the homeless in the next chapter, and the opportunity they represent for us to grow in compassion and love. Here suffice it to say that usually I am open to giving money away when people ask me or when they present a particular need.

I feel no real attachment to money, property, and possessions. I don't allow them to rule me or even to preoccupy me in any way. I know the value of a dollar, but I'm not obsessed with this value, because I realize that other factors in my life are far more valuable. We all know there is an emptiness in the goods of this world. Many of us lust after some possession, only to feel a nagging emptiness once we attain it. We try to ignore this emptiness, thinking that the next object will somehow fill us. But it never does. The more money we make, the more money we want, always thinking that satisfaction is just around the bend. Perhaps this is why many celebrities who have attained fantastic wealth turn to the practice of Buddhism, with its emphasis on nonattachment. They have realized that money doesn't bring happiness or inner peace.

The emptiness of things has a lot to do with their impermanence, once we realize it. In Buddhism, as in Christianity, and actually as in most traditions, this emptiness comes from the awareness that possessions don't last and can be ours only temporarily. When we realize, furthermore, that there are more ultimate values that are indeed permanent, then the intrinsic insufficiency of material objects and money strikes us in our guts. We are seeking something we must find elsewhere. I know that worldly goods can never substitute for the Divine itself. My awareness of the Divine is the absolute center of my will and deepest aspirations, though I often fail in my human frailty.

That said, money can make a tremendous difference in the lives of those who don't have enough for basic necessities. I have always felt, for as long as I've reflected on this issue, that money and other resources are to be shared, that the reason some people have more than others is to help their brothers and sisters in need. Sharing with others is incumbent on all of us, no matter how modest our income may be. I am convinced that we have a responsibility to try to do what we can with what we've got. The more a person has, the greater his or her responsibility to make something available for others, and not only for members of one's family or one's circle of friends. We must heed the sobering words of Jesus: How easy it is to love those who love you, or whom you easily love, but how much harder it is to love those whom don't love you or who you wouldn't ordinarily choose to love.

A new spirit of service, a new kind of philanthropy, is alive in America. This was certainly shown by the outpouring of love and money spurred by the devastating events of September 11,

2001. But this spirit of service had awakened before that, as many people became aware of the gross inequities that our prosperity was creating. An anonymous donor gave seventy-five million dollars to the Salvation Army a few years ago. Ted Turner donated a billion dollars to the United Nations, a real shock to many in the upper class. It never dawned on some of them that with wealth comes a responsibility to share it. When Turner gave his money to the U.N., he set an example, perhaps even a standard. Many billionaires have subsequently established foundations to distribute grants to worthy people and causes. In 2001 Gordon Moore, the cofounder of Intel, with his wife, Betty, donated a staggering $6.13 billion, while Bill and Melinda Gates donated $2 billion. We have still a long way to go in this area of charity, but change is apparent.

The spiritual man or woman, the mystic in society, is of course subject to the culture's influence. But with spiritual maturity comes the realization that the value of money is ultimately not economic but spiritual. Its spiritual value comes from what it makes possible in one's development, opportunities for self-transcendence it creates when we reach out to others, responding to their needs, being there for them in needy moments. Life continually presents us with a choice: either to seek for ourselves or to think of others, to feather our own nests or to be concerned with others who suffer from want.

THE SPIRITUAL PERSPECTIVE

Only spirituality can give us the awareness of how to use our resources wisely — where we can realize the maximum benefit for others as well as ourselves. Spirituality, in this sense, means consciousness, the requisite awareness to distinguish between the real and the unreal. Through commitment to the inner life we become progressively more conscious, more aware of what's actually important. Awareness has to be worked at; it doesn't just happen. Although people experience divine interventions from time to time, resulting in increased perception of what's ultimately real, normally each one of us must work at it every day of our earthly sojourn.

The spiritual life offers us perspective on time, work, money, and other resources — on their real roles. It shows us their place and reduces our capacity to deceive ourselves about them. It demands clarity of us, the illumination of truth. We cannot live for our job or for our possessions. We are certainly not masters of time, but in many ways its victims. We are not really in charge. Western culture is so concerned about control, or I should say the illusion of control, since we actually have none, except of our own will. The spiritual journey reveals this insight to us again and again. Most of our experiences are encounters with our limitations, and life keeps providing opportunities to learn this lesson: We are not in control; we only think we are.

A profoundly important part of the spiritual life is to use time, our work or career, and our resources wisely, often a long journey in itself. Gaining this wisdom is our own choice, our decision to be in the world but not possessed by it or obsessed over it. To be in the world but not of it — this is the perspective that allows us to value time, career, and resources with genuine understanding. It is a way to keep our world in order, a way springing from the perennial sources of spirituality that arise as vigorous currents of the world's religions. Spiritual teachers throughout history have realized and taught this way of keeping our world in order: Brother David Steindl-Rast and Father Thomas Keating in our own time, the *rishis* and the Buddha in

India, Zoroaster in Persia, Lao-tzu in China, the prophets of Israel, Jesus of Nazareth, the prophet Muhammad. All have contributed dramatically to the process of transformation in the spiritual life of the planet. We need all their voices, all their visions, particularly as we attempt to live a spiritual life in the world.

CHAPTER 6

Light in the Streets

The Urgent Call of the Homeless

In a rather depressing cartoon, a rotund, wealthy man walking up a New York avenue comes across three homeless people, each staking out a different street corner. On encountering the first, he yells at him, "Get a job!" The homeless man is, needless to say, a little taken aback. Then the wealthy man rounds the corner and bumps into the second homeless gentleman, to whom he blurts, "Get a grip!" Like the first, the second man is startled by this assault. The wealthy man continues past him up the avenue and meets the third homeless man. He saunters over to him, enjoying his sense of power and control, and bellows in his face: "Get a life, you scum!" With a smug sense of satisfaction, the rich man keeps walking, happy with the advice he's delivered to these people who contribute "nothing" to society. After walking a few more blocks, he turns another corner and runs directly into the three homeless men standing together. Surrounding him, they firmly yet gently remind him: "Get a heart!"

The presence of the homeless poor in every big American city occasions fear, indifference, anger, and in many, compassion. Some respond to them, acquiescing to their requests; others verbally accost them, feeling burdened by their constant beseeching. Some people, overwhelmed by their suffering, don't want to see the homeless; they avert their eyes, pretending the homeless don't exist. Many of us are frightened to look into their eyes, because to do so brings home how close their plight is to our own. While most of us enjoy a strong safety net of friends and family, perhaps some of us are just a lost job or a nervous breakdown away from joining them. But to look carries with it responsibility for what you see — in this case poor people, trapped in tragic circumstances.

This simple cartoon depicts the huge chasm between our society's most fortunate and the least fortunate as well as our great need for a change in our perspective. This truly is an issue concerning the heart — its maturity and depth — and our willingness to love and be compassionate, kind, healing, and merciful to everyone, but especially to the most vulnerable, our marginalized street people. The homeless dramatically represent capitalism's failures, shown not just on the dry pages of our newspapers but in real people we see every day. But they also present an everyday opportunity for us truly to *practice* our spirituality, to see, as Mother Teresa did, the face of Jesus in the sickest and most destitute.

I have made it one of the central goals of my practice not just to notice these people, but to engage them, for that is how we see beyond the old dialectic between us, those who feel we follow the rules, and *them*, the people on the street who cannot or seemingly choose not to. When we get to know them, we realize that the situation is much more complicated, that our society doesn't provide much leeway for human frailties. In this chapter I will briefly tell the stories of a number of home-less people I know and have known for years. I will relate my way of responding to them, present some of the powerful lessons we can learn from them, and show some of the concrete programs for them that emphasize a human approach, a compassionate, loving heart.

THE OMNIPRESENCE OF THE HOMELESS

The homeless live in virtually every city and town around the globe, representing a sixth of humanity — or about a billion souls. Like ghosts, they haunt the busy thoroughfares of the world. And like the lepers of old — who sadly still exist in India and elsewhere — the homeless are outcasts, almost nonpeople. Yet every street person has a name, a history, a family. Each one has dreams, aspirations, fears, and expectations. All have known incredible suffering and rejection and a sense of help-less desperation. Some of them endure mental illness and many different kinds of physical pathology, and most of them suffer from addiction, an ailment for which our society has little patience. All of them try to scrape out a meager living in the heart of our cities by begging or by selling newspapers.

The homeless poor are destitute of material goods and in many cases have little formal education. Although there is a wide spectrum among street people, I view them all as essentially refugees from capitalism, as victims of the system's basic inequity. Mother Teresa often remarked, "We have the poor because we don't share!" And yet her life was an eloquent witness not simply to sharing what she had but also to loving the poor, the seemingly unlovable. These were the people she chose to cherish. Rescuing the dying — the elderly, the middle-aged, children, and infants — represents only one small part of her charity and service to broken and vulnerable humanity.

Surely we need more people with Mother Teresa's awareness, capacity, and generosity of heart. The Gospel inspired her work; she put the Gospel into action, love into action.

The cold facts of capitalism are an unwillingness to share and a lack of social responsibility. Individuals may exhibit this responsibility, but the system itself ignores it. We must face the fact that capitalism doesn't have a heart; rather it has broken billions of hearts, particularly in developing countries. Pope John Paul II has been critical of this inhuman tendency of capitalism and has advocated its reform all during his long pontificate. The reform of capitalism is a problem for all of us, not just CEOs, board members, and stockholders, because we all have a stake in this system. And we are all responsible. Many of us have grown prosperous with little thought to the consequences for others. Part of this reform is becoming educated about our economic institutions. This education really means becoming committed to a solution for homelessness and paying attention to the plight of the masses of poor who exist almost everywhere.

In America, though homelessness already existed, it became an endemic, tragic fact during the Reagan, Bush, and Clinton eras. Although there are no precise figures, and estimates vary considerably, the number of homeless in America alone is somewhere between 300,000 to 750,000. I think the number is much higher. I have heard in the Chicago area alone there are around eighty thousand. New York Governor Nelson Rockefeller contributed to the growth of this problem, just as Reagan did as governor of California, with his heartless policy of dumping poor mentally ill persons from state-operated asylums into the streets.

And there are many less visible actions against homeless people as well. Something many take for granted and never question but that has had a devastating impact on the homeless is the phenomenon of condominium conversion. These schemes seem innocent, but their results are quite destructive to the poor of our cities living in subsidized housing. Most of these buildings are increasingly taken over by developers and converted into condominiums. These units are rarely ever replaced. The end result is that the poor are consigned to the streets. This pattern has been repeated again and again in every part of North America.

The situation in Chicago is fairly typical of most other cities: The homeless are pushed to the margins. Chicago's Lower Wacker Drive, a partially underground street along the edge of the city's Loop, has been for years a haven for hundreds of homeless women, men, and their children. Lower Wacker provided basic shelter and warmth from Chicago's frightfully cold winters with the residual heat of surrounding buildings, near which the homeless poor would eat and sleep. Caring souls would come by with food, blankets, and other necessities. Mayor Richard Daley moved against them and ordered the removal of these hundreds of street people from the relative shelter of Lower Wacker. The mayor has tried to cope with the problem, but the city's shelter system is stretched to the limit and cannot meet the growing demand.

Another action aimed at the homeless in Chicago also occurred as a result of one of the mayor's decisions. For years the homeless would ride the Blue Line to O'Hare Airport. The Blue Line is a subway, also called the "L." Many of them would also find a remote part of the airport that wasn't being used, or the tunnel, to sleep in and get warm. Mayor Daley put a stop to these practices and prevented the homeless from coming to the airport. Many of them are harassed on the Blue Line, and yet a few still ride the subway to keep warm and enjoy some respite from the cold. Some continue to beg on these trains, even though there are periodic announcements that "soliciting on the Blue Line is strictly forbidden, and violators will be arrested." The mayor felt compelled to take this action because airport commuters were constantly being pressured for money from the more aggressive members of the homeless society riding the trains or taking refuge in the airport. He saw a threat to the local economy from a too-visible and too-active homeless population.

Some Encounters with the Homeless

Over the years I have come to know many street people. Some are mentally ill; others are con artists. Most of these people are decent and simply want a second chance. The homeless poor I introduce here represent only a small number of the homeless people I have known, but their examples are sufficient for providing insight into their difficult but fascinating world.

Carol

Carol was a white woman in her fifties I knew for about seven years. She was thin, pale, and malnourished. Usually she stood by Union Station, on Adams Street where one of the main commuter trains for the surrounding Chicago area arrives and departs, asking the steady stream of passengers for donations. Although she wasn't homeless, she was very poor and ill. Some technicality disqualified her from complete disability payments, and she was reduced to begging on the streets. After I had known her for several years, I found her standing at her usual spot weeping. I inquired what was wrong, and she told me a strange story.

It seems there was a swimming competition in the canal next to where Carol stood. Whoever could swim across the canal and back the fastest would win a thousand dollars. Several had entered the race, and while she was watching the various swimmers line up, a man turned to her and said: "Why don't you jump in, and win the money?" Carol responded, "But I can't swim." He turned back to the water and said flatly, "Why don't you just jump in anyway?" Most people are more aware and compassionate than this man, but his remark is symptomatic of widespread feeling that people who don't contribute to society in conventional ways are useless.

The day came when Carol was gone, and I haven't seen her in some time. I remember her as a cheerful person who would play her harmonica for passersby. Commuters would stop to chat and give her a dollar. I found her to be a good human being who simply, through some combination of ailments and circumstances, couldn't fit the narrowly defined channels of what we consider acceptable members of society. She once told me about an old aunt who lived with her, who needed to move to a drier climate. Carol was saving money for this move. I imagine they eventually did make it to Arizona, and I hope that now their life is easier.

The "Saint"

The other six examples of street people I present here are all African American, as are most of the homeless poor in Chicago. One of them is a man in his mid-fifties who calls himself the "Saint." He is tall and slender, with a kindly face. I don't know his real name, but every time I meet him — usually in Hyde Park, where I live — he walks up to me and says: "Hi, I'm a saint, and I need two dollars. Can you help me?" Well, what can you say to a presentation like that? It's certainly original, though from my Catholic perspective, I normally leave that kind of proclamation to others!

I don't know much about the Saint, but he possesses charm and innocence, an unusual sense of abandon and trust, as if he has seen something important. He doesn't seem to worry very much, and I find him easy to engage in conversation, although it's difficult to get much out of him. He doesn't talk a lot about himself or his mysterious background. I find this true of many street people; they never tell you much about themselves, only what they need to share with you at the time. It has always impressed me that the Saint is never greedy. Some street people give the impression that you can never help them enough. We need to be discerning, and when we encounter this grasping attitude, we should perhaps resist it, depending on the situation.

Jerome

Jerome lives on the stairs to the Metra train at Fifty-third Street on Chicago's south side. This is where I met him six years ago while climbing the same stairs to catch the train downtown. As I walked up these stairs and looked up, there he was, the most interesting street person I know, mostly because of his desire to contribute to society in his way. He has considerable wisdom that stems from his desire to help and even protect others. He perceives one of his purposes to be the protection of passengers who pass through his station on Fifty-third Street. He tells me the police allow him to sleep on the steps because he's a good presence there.

At around forty, Jerome looks healthy. He's rugged, and he eats regularly through the generosity of a few local restaurant owners. He spends a good part of each day, hour after hour, just walking around the neighborhood. His face has become windburned from its exposure to the elements. He claims to own a house in Canada and one in Georgia, with a large

income to sustain him, but he says certain people have inter-
fered with his life and are preventing him from obtaining what
is rightly his. I don't know which of his numerous stories to
believe, but I like him because he has a very good heart.

Frank

Then there's Frank. He is very tall and thin, a gentle man in
his late forties with a ready smile. Every time I encounter
Frank, he asks me if I have any work for him. When I answer
him that I don't, since I don't own any property, he starts to
cry. He tells me he wants to work, but he can never find a job,
that no one will give him a chance. I do what I can for Frank
when I see him, as I do for all the others, but he is more of a
challenge, because he frequently shows what can only be
called a whiny quality. When things are not going his way, he
turns on the tears. It's very manipulative, but it's his method
of survival. His tears have brought him through many difficult situations.

Frank is a born-again Christian, and at times he's quite
vocal about spreading his version of the Gospel. When he
becomes evangelical, I find conversations with him tedious. I
appreciate his faith, the genuineness of his commitment, and
the purity of his intention, but his fervor is sometimes a bit
much. But along with his tears, his faith has served him well; it
seems to be the bedrock on which his life is grounded.

Milton

Milton is always on the same corner. He stands in front of a
Starbuck's on the corner of Harper and Fifty-third Street, not
far from Jerome's abode at the Metra Station. Milton is a very
simple man, gentle and friendly. He is most likely in his late
forties. All the people in the neighborhood like him and show

him consistent kindness. The staff at Starbuck's are extremely supportive of Milton, giving him coffee, scones, and sandwiches. Milton has a sweet disposition, though I feel he smokes too much for his own good. He is an even-tempered person, with a consistent presence and energy. His serenity is awesome. Whenever I pass by his corner, we talk for a bit; I give him a dollar and encourage him in any way I can.

Sometimes when I'm walking down the opposite side of the street, deep in thought, Milton will spot me, call to me, and then run across the street to talk with me, and of course, to get his dollar. There is something childlike and amusing about Milton's approach. He knows what he wants, and he goes after it, unconcerned with what others might think. While I find Milton's perseverance endearing, some might find his personality a challenge, like that of most homeless people who have some personality trait that prevents them from holding down work. In other societies, such marginal characters are often kept within the communty's fold; they find a place with relatives, friends, or a benefactor. Our version of community is less forgiving.

Peggy

One of the most fascinating street people I've ever known is Peggy because of her sheer gall. Peggy is around forty-five and has a hard edge to her looks and character. She has a small apartment that's subsidized by the city of Chicago, but she has very little income. She has several children, some of them very small. Peggy also has been a drug addict, and I'm never sure if she's still using. She says she's not, but I can't tell for certain. She can be very manipulative. I have learned over the years in working with street people to be discerning. I can usually sense when she's handing me a story.

Although Peggy wants very much to have a job, if for

nothing other than her self-respect, she never seems able to get one. She has many problems, and some of these are related to her health and her children. I talk to her about once a week. She comes around, and I give her some money. I've noticed in the years I've known Peggy that she's never satisfied, whereas the other street people I know are usually very grateful. Of all the people I know on the street, I worry the most over her and her children. She is extremely impatient with them and doesn't hesitate to yell at them over minor provocations. If she makes a wrong turn, she could ruin their lives. I'm not sure how aware she is of her responsibility. Every time I meet her, I try to see her need objectively and then respond appropriately. All in all, Peggy presents quite a challenge. Thankfully, she now has a part-time job in a day care center and is slowing inching her way into a more conventional life.

Wilma

Wilma is another matter. At about fifty years old, Wilma has a wonderful sense of humor and a kind heart. She can always be found on Jackson Street between Wabash and Michigan Avenues. This is her turf. Whenever I see her, I always give her a hug. Ever happy and singing, Wilma has a wonderful way of lifting your spirits. Wilma is a vendor for *Street Wise*, a weekly newspaper for the homeless, which she sells every day.

One very telling incident demonstrates her big heart: Once as I was out walking, I spotted Wilma conversing with a poor white family. Apparently, this family was destitute, stranded in Chicago with no money. Wilma had collected about forty-five dollars that day, and she gave it all to them, to rescue them from the streets until they could return to their home in downstate Springfield. To see this woman's compassion with these vulnerable souls, and to witness her generosity, gave me tremendous joy. Wilma taught me a profound lesson about the homeless: There are often saints among their ranks.[1]

People so often judge the poor, accusing them of being lazy, manipulative, and exploitative. Some of them are, but not all of them. The ones who are need direction and encouragement. Those that aren't need our understanding and help. Wilma seems like such an exception, but I feel she is not that rare; there are many Wilmas. We just have to look and have faith in humanity. Sometimes people judge the homeless so they can dismiss them and justify their lack of response. If street people are seen simply as con artists too lazy to work, then it's easier to walk away. It's painful to look at the poor, and even more demanding to interact with them, as some of the above stories illustrate. Doing so, it becomes impossible to escape the sense of responsibility that builds within our individual and collective conscience.

FACING YOUR INNER LEPER

My own reactions to the homeless poor have gone through an evolution. From annoyance, resentment, and inconvenience to spontaneous compassion, my feelings about them have steadily developed. Sometimes I have tried to avoid them, but in the city they are practically on every corner. Everywhere one turns, panhandlers stand like guards on duty. For a while I would simply give money in an almost perfunctory manner and not really engage them or actually see them for who they are. But as time went on, and after seemingly endless encounters, I realized that these people are precious, that I was missing something important, something essential I must face squarely.

Like St. Francis of Assisi, I had to face my own inner leper, my own fear of the vulnerability I saw in these souls. St. Francis found lepers repugnant. He knew he had to accept them and love them, but they repulsed him. He experienced an almost visceral reaction to them. Then one day as Francis was on his way to a new town to preach, he saw a leper in the distance ringing a bell. "Unclean, get away," the leper shouted. "I'm unclean." Francis approached him, embraced him, and kissed him on the lips. In these acts he conquered his fear. That night he had a vivid dream. The leper appeared to him, and it was Christ!

I began to look deeply into the eyes of all the street people I met. I began to see them on a much subtler level. I began to see Spirit, Christ, or God in them. Although it's usually never convenient when we meet the poor — the Gospel is not about convenience, but about love in every situation — it is crucial for us to respond in some way from our hearts. I understood the homeless are a test of our humanity, and a test of each one of us who has this opportunity given to them. I also realized I had to do something.

I am not usually the type to found organizations and programs, nor am I much of an administrator. I prefer to approach the problem unsystematically and spontaneously, as I encounter street people. My work with them is a quiet, personal response, not a public program. Unorganized, but deeply committed, I reach out to the homeless as I meet them. In time, some of these people have become an important part of my life, and I couldn't conceive of my life being any other way. These precious souls have greatly enriched me with their unique personalities, their wisdom, and humor. They have deepened my understanding of the meaning of our time here on this precious planet.

The various reactions to the poor that I've experienced are, I think, fairly typical. Living an intense and comprehensive spiritual life as a monastic is no guarantee that one's attitude will be more enlightened. Three Catholic monks in Chicago during the Parliament of the World's Religions in 1993 taught me this vividly. Although I mentioned this incident in my book *The Mystic Heart,* it is so appropriate and ironic, it bears repeating here.[2]

Two of these three monks were Benedictine, and one was a Trappist. I know all three very well; one told me the story because it had so disturbed him. They were walking to their car from the hotel where the sessions of the Parliament were held. As they walked, the Trappist was presenting an idea about service to the homeless, expanding on the talk they had just participated in, while the other two listened. As they got deeply into their discussion, a street person lying prostrate on the pavement began to call to them. Two of them continued the conversation, taking no notice of the man, even though it was impossible to miss his presence. The younger of the monks looked long at the homeless man, who was obviously in distress and need. He wanted to do something, at least to talk to the poor soul, but he didn't know how to approach him. The monk was himself a bit of an introvert, and he realized that he'd never received any teaching in his monastery about the demands of compassion, how to move from theory to action.

This is a common problem for most of us. It requires a mature spirituality to respond in such situations. These three monks are all compassionate people, but they'd lived for so many years isolated from the world's deepest suffering that they didn't know what to do. The problem of homelessness is not something they have to deal with, as most of us don't. We need to learn how to respond, and that's where wisdom must guide our essentially compassionate natures.

LIGHT ON THE STREETS: EVOLVING A CARING HEART

In developing compassion, begin with the realization that all sentient beings want to be happy and avoid suffering, as the

Dalai Lama often reminds us. Just as we each want to be happy and free of pain, anxiety, and illness, so do all the people we meet. This is just as true of street people as it is of us. They want so much to be happy, to be liberated from their condition. Very few of them have chosen to be homeless and alone. Circumstances have conspired to bring them to their unfortunate situation. Tender commiseration is the beginning of growing the compassionate heart, which we all have, if only we could allow ourselves the freedom to live out of this deeper, more ultimate nature we all have in common.

One simple but effective way to develop compassion is to *intend* it each day — to think of it and reflect on its nature as part of you, part of all of us. Our compassion is a fruit of our spiritual lives; it actually arises spontaneously when formed by intention in our spiritual practice. Love and compassion are always the goods of the spiritual journey, and they are guided by divine wisdom, which then shapes compassion in the concrete situations of our existence. Compassion, love, mercy, and kindness are the attributes of our true and common nature when we become freed from social conditioning and the indifference that often accompanies ignorance. The mystical life awakens knowledge of our genuine nature; it is a path to who we really are. The more we pursue it honestly, the more we become aware of our innate love and compassion.

Another effective way to realize our compassionate nature is through suffering. A divorce, the death of a loved one, a serious illness, a broken heart — all these put us into contact with our deeper nature and thus open our hearts to others' suffering and vulnerability. To learn from suffering, we have to be open to it, to allow it to shape our other-centeredness. (I will consider suffering, illness, and healing further in chapter 8 and connect it to the spiritual journey itself.)

Compassion, or what the Christian tradition has called charity, a translation of *agape*, the selfless, divine love of the Gospel — what Jesus exemplified and taught — is the avenue to understanding the vulnerability, marginality, and sufferings of the homeless and other street poor. Compassion allows us to see what may not be immediately obvious: the basic needs of the street people, the needs that are also our needs for food, clothing, and medical protection as well as for affirmation, acceptance, and a sense of home.

Basic temporalities are more obvious — while affirmation, acceptance, and a sense of home may not be. But they become more obvious as we engage homeless people in real conversation. When we look into the eyes of a man or woman on the street we perceive their fundamental need for affirmation. Everyone wants his or her story heard. To affirm others, especially those who are suffering, in need, or desperate, is to proclaim their value, their worth, and especially their worthiness of love. They must be affirmed, as all of us must. Like the rest of us, the homeless want to be seen, affirmed, and accepted.

In the cartoon about the heartless rich man and the three street people we can discern the problem with this man's attitude. He is inwardly dead, in a state of ignorance that disconnects him from his ultimate nature: his compassion, love, kindness, and mercy. He is so absorbed in himself, in his wealth, in the ease of his life that he could neither see nor accept the suffering of those three people. He relied on social notions of what's right, the roles people are supposed to play in society, and he closed himself off to the reality of their lives. He missed a precious opportunity to grow. Of course this was only a cartoon, but one with truth behind it, reflecting many people's attitudes.

In our encounters with the poor, as with anyone, we need to

show that we accept them. Acceptance appears in our willingness to be present to them, not simply to pass them by or give them money to get rid of them. If we give them money in a perfunctory manner, they will know it. Often this seems like what they want, but we are then passing an opportunity to exchange spirit through conversation, through opening our hearts to them, through really listening deeply and with commiseration.

In addition to affirmation and acceptance, the homeless poor desperately need a sense of home, that is, to actually *have* a home, even a room, which they can enter, close the door to, and live in peace. Just as all of us thrive in the sanctuary of our own homes, the homeless need not just a shelter, a room in another's house, but their own space. This insight seems very basic, but considering this point with compassion reveals its deep truth. A home represents security, the security of being free of the vagaries of the street, the noise and occasional violence of shelters, and the indifference of the world. With a true home comes a sense of protection, well-being, and hope. Reflect on all the qualities of home for you, what your home means to you, your family, and friends, and then by extension apply those insights to the street people.

Although they will never entirely solve the problem, many individual projects and shelters make tremendous inroads into the suffering of the homeless. In Evanston, Illinois, north of Chicago, a forward-looking faith community called Lake Street Church is trying to address the needs of the homeless. The pastor of this Baptist community, the Reverend Robert Thompson, is also the chairman of the Parliament of the World's Religions. His church welcomes members from any tradition, not just Christians, and has a fourteen-year-old fully functioning facility for the homeless, which houses thirty-two people every night, 365 days a year. The Lake Street Church strives to give the people who stay there a sense of security, home, peace, and well-being. It looks after all their needs, including medical treatment, but always strives to prepare them to return to a normal life rather than creating dependence. The people staying there receive counseling, practice job interviews, and training. They are given transitional housing and gentle supervision while they slowly integrate back into regular life. The approach of the Lake Street Church is imaginative and socially responsible. It indicates the kind of response that is possible when people get in touch with their intrinsic compassion.

Another wonderful program for economically marginalized people is a center in Seattle run by the Catholic Church. The Archdiocese of Seattle bought a huge old hotel downtown and has invited street people to live there. More than a shelter, it strives to offer real independence for approximately five hundred residents. They all have their own rooms, can have a phone, and can eat in the facility's cafeteria. Most of the people fortunate enough to be residents have jobs, usually secured with the help of the facility's staff members. Most of their rents are subsidized. This hotel serves a great function, stimulating concern and response from the more fortunate.

Obviously, there are many programs for the homeless, including thousands of soup kitchens and shelters run by generous, dedicated souls, but the Catholic Worker Movement founded by Dorothy Day and her community in the 1930s represents a significant advance in understanding their situation and finding a solution to it. Catholic Worker Houses exist in the major cities of America.[3] They are based on her Mary and Joseph Houses on the Lower East Side of Manhattan, where she would personally welcome the homeless.

Day's unique contribution was to embrace the homeless in

her own home, in total vulnerability to them and with them. She allowed them to live with her and her community, letting them take up every space possible, and always making room for others who came along. "If every family took in one homeless person, then there would be no problem of homelessness," she would often say, echoing Mother Teresa's views. The generosity of permitting others in need to live with us is a giant step forward in responding to this difficult issue. Her approach opens a space within our hearts, overcoming the false dichotomy that distinguishes these souls from us and it celebrates the intrinsic interdependence among us all.

The vision of my former community, Hundred Acres Monastery in New Hampshire, which existed from 1964 to 1992, was in many ways similar to the Catholic Worker communities in its sensitivity and openness to the homeless. In fact, I often have thought that Hundred Acres was a Catholic Worker house in "slow motion" — it definitely had its spirit, though in a rural setting and with only a few street people living there. Overall, we strived to welcome everyone who came to our door. This openness and welcoming attitude was initiated by the founder of the community, Father Paul Fitzgerald, a Trappist monk.

Father Paul's mission of opening the monastery to the homeless began one night in the mid-sixties, around midnight, when a German teenage girl came to the monastery door, knocking loudly and urgently. Father Paul got out of bed to answer it and found the poor girl terribly distraught, crying and irrational. She had just broken up with her American boyfriend and had no place to go. "Can I stay for a day or two, please?" she pleaded through her tears. Father Paul looked at her with great empathy and welcomed her, saying: "Please, let me show you to your room!" Father Paul was willing to live the

Gospel, and he did, just like Mother Teresa, Dorothy Day, and countless others. Father Paul's loving acceptance had wonderful results. The girl, who without a place to stay might have been victim to suicide, rape, or other injury, went on to thrive in the United States and became a successful businesswoman.

What Do the Homeless Teach Us?

In my growing appreciation for the homeless, I have come to believe that people living on the street have a lot to offer us: profound insights gleaned as we process our experiences with them. Although they are not intentionally our teachers and most likely don't realize the insight into life they offer, they can offer us deep understandings about life. Unwittingly, simply through their difficult position, they perform a vital function. They may not intend to be our teachers, but the poor grant us a unique perspective on life we cannot find elsewhere.

What is it that they can teach us? They remind us of the impermanence of this existence and how attached we are to what passes away. We have so much, and when confronted with people who have nothing — who are vulnerable, helpless, and destitute — we receive their help in overcoming fear and insecurity. The poor hold this power — the power of truth itself. When we respond in love instead of fear, when we don't ignore them but instead see them and consider their condition, are we not reminded of our own ultimate fragility and tentativeness as beings in this world?

Of course, we fear the loss of basic security the condition of the homeless represents. It's a forced loss of attachment, a nonpossessiveness they have no choice about, at least in the beginning. Each moment of a street person's life is taken up with survival, and we become the key to that pursuit. Their situation of being stripped of everything is too painful for most of us to look at. We much prefer to hide in the shadows of a questionable happiness, in our comfortable abundance. Whenever we see a street person, these insecurities and fears surface, like spirits in the night.

The homeless, quite unconsciously, draw our attention to our grasping nature, how we are always pursuing acquisition of more and more things, of power and position, of property and money. If we can prevent ourselves from succumbing to our natural weakness and fear by turning away, they force us to think of our position. They also compel us to see society's gross inequity. More basically still, they prove the truth of the Gospel, which tells us that people are more important than money and property. They allow us to understand how foolishly we pursue things that are useless if we fail in the ways of compassion, love, kindness, and mercy. The poor, through their quiet presence in the streets and elsewhere, continually call us to reflect on our priorities.

Their impoverishment ultimately reminds us of our own poverty of existence and time, that this life is impermanent, regardless of how much we embellish it with wealth. When we are separated from all the goods of this world, we are no different from our homeless brothers and sisters. Even without economic, social, and educational equality, there is an inescapable existential equality among us all. In the late 1980s, India's tragically impoverished inspired me to reflect on what was really essential in my life. These poor souls — poor economically, though rich culturally, spiritually, and humanly — taught me a profound lesson, one I've never forgotten. The homeless poor are everywhere on the subcontinent, and I noticed in the vast majority of them that, though destitute and possessing nothing, they were happy and serene beyond comprehension, a serenity connected with their faith, not their poverty! They taught me that one needs very little to be happy, that happiness is a spiritual quality that has absolutely nothing to do with wealth and possessions. This critical lesson is, of course, universally valid.

Simplicity and Sharing

The overwhelming poverty and homelessness around the globe demand of us all a new direction, one founded on true economic, social, and political justice for everyone. But this justice has a very personal reality for us, not just a political or social one, which is based on two vital principles: simplicity and sharing.

The principles of sharing and simplicity are inspired by loving compassion, kindness, mercy, and a highly refined sensitivity that allows us to see their necessity. This sensitivity is the gift, indeed the grace, of the spiritual life. The more than six billion members of the human family now inhabiting the earth, like all who have preceded us and all who will come after, are part of an interdependent community of sentience and life. This reality cries out to our sense of justice, inspiring us to oppose poverty and homelessness.

The Dalai Lama often observes that we human beings have a universal responsibility for the earth and all its suffering. The truth of this insight I realize more and more in the depths of my own conscience. We all have the task of living a simpler lifestyle that allows resources to become available and distributed more equitably. Simplicity means taking just what we need and nothing more. It translates into living with far less, so that everyone will have something. It requires a process of reducing desires and carefully identifying legitimate needs.

If we change the way we live, if we actually simplify our existence in our time and around the world, then it will be possible truly to share with one another. Sensitive sharing leads us to discern the needs of others whenever we encounter them. As higher sentient beings, we are meant to share with others. Although we may recognize our root biological tendency to horde and fight for our survival, that basic tendency is not what makes us human — overcoming that tendency is. Unfortunately, most people don't realize the truth simply because of their social conditioning, which blocks them from the awareness of their responsibility to act compassionately all the time, regardless of the situation. By sharing and by simplifying our lives we can restore balance to the system we inherited from our predecessors. We can replace our self-serving culture with a compassionate one that takes into account the interdependent reality of which we are all part.

Street people present us with both a problem and an opportunity: a problem in terms of the immense dimensions of this tragedy, and an opportunity in terms of the possibility of developing our innate loving kindness for them. As long as we ignore the homeless or apply a Band-Aid solution to the symptoms of a much larger disorder in our world, the problem will grow and finally get out of control. The reality of homelessness alerts us to the need to transform the whole global system, to build a new civilization in which this terrible agony of so many no longer exists.

Toward a Permanent Solution

A genuine solution to this massive social ill will necessitate a new order of civilization — a civilization with a heart, a compassionate, kind, loving, and merciful universal social order. In time capitalism will have to be transformed, and this will happen as more and more people wake up to the deeper reality of which we are all equal members. Corporate executives, employees, and stockholders all have the capacity for such an awakening. It's only a matter of time — if we have the necessary leadership. Our leadership, particularly with respect to the homeless problem, needs a special kind of guidance, that of our spiritual communities themselves.

We must have a mobilized effort involving all churches, synagogues, mosques, and temples — all the communities of the world's great religions. Our spiritual leaders are in a position to concentrate the minds of the masses on the great tragedy of homelessness. Just as Martin Luther King Jr., with the help of the churches, was able to coordinate the Civil Rights movement, our spiritual leaders can bring the homeless situation to the forefront. Our spiritual leaders are capable of bringing a new sense of conscience to the popular imagination about the seriousness of this crisis, inspiring a change of direction for our society. What was done in the 1960s and 1970s for civil rights can be done in our time for homelessness and other forms of poverty.

As a monk, a mystic in the world, pursuing my spiritual practice each day, I have awakened to the horrible inequity in the sufferings of the homeless persons I have known for so long. I have realized it is no good depending on an often uneven approach of providing shelters and soup kitchens. We must call on something much more ambitious to transform this problem. We can create such a world, but it demands will and determination; it won't just happen without the insight, leadership, and the mobilization of a movement.

Contemplatives, mystics, and monastics are by nature countercultural. They are in touch, through desire, vision, and experience, with something ultimate. Their understanding of reality and value arises from the Source. Their perceptions and estimation of society, of the world, always put them in conflict with the world's illusions, or more precisely with the illusions most people entertain about themselves, their desires, and hidden agendas.

A monk or mystic contemplative in the mainstream of society is an agent of change, of reform. He or she has a vision of a human world animated by the best qualities of which we are capable, a world where compassion is alive, where love takes precedence over indifference, kindness over neglect, and mercy over oppression. Mystics in the heart of society are a source of radical reform, radical in the original meaning of the Latin root *radex,* which means going to the root. The reform I have in mind is the most radical of all: the eventual disappearance of cultural and economic selfishness, and their replacement with sharing, compassionate concern, loving kindness, and merciful consideration of all. In such a new world street people will find a real home and the opportunities to cultivate themselves and their God-given gifts, thus allowing their innate preciousness to shine forth.

CHAPTER 7

Dancing on the Edge

The Struggle to Promote Change

Change is one of the most difficult human dilemmas. We all are drawn to stability and security, and we all struggle with transition. Change represents a threat to our world, a break from the comfort of routine, and we are in many ways biologically wired to resist it. And yet change, when brought about with intelligence and wisdom, is precisely what our planet needs: in business, in education and the arts, in the religions, in science, in politics, in economics, in our relationship with the earth.

A mystic in society, through spiritual practice and practical interactions with the world, gains an enlarged perspective on the fundamental nature of justice and on what is needed to transform long-standing problems. A mystic in the world also focuses on the necessity to inform others of the issues required by reform and of the fundamental changes that will bring about genuine human progress. This evolution of the human spirit is a shift from narrow interests to ones springing from a deeper ground of awareness and compassion, of selfless love, kindness, and mercy.

Transforming consciousness on our planet requires us to stretch beyond local and private interests to more universal issues — issues that force growth and change. This work toward growth, and ultimately toward justice, has been a very concrete focus in my life and bears a direct relationship to *conscientization*, the awakening of a deeper awareness of problems that require of us some kind of response, especially when people are suffering. One primary issue for me, and the focus of this chapter, is how the Catholic Church, the interfaith movement (particularly in the Parliament of the World's Religions), and the United Nations all address the struggle of the Tibetan people. My own efforts in this struggle expand into a general effort toward pluralism and peace and toward bringing to bear the responsibility of world religions to work together for a lasting global peace. I don't take any credit for effecting great change with these issues, but I try to make them an integral part of my life work, a natural outgrowth of my practice.

UNDERSTANDING THE NATURE OF JUSTICE

Although we all have a sense of what constitutes true justice, few of us attempt a deeper look at it. Our perspective is almost always filtered through social conditioning from family, school, and society. Most often, the cultural conveyer of our information about the world is television and the movies, which communicate a simplified version of things, always within the context of our capitalist system.

Most of us have an elementary grasp of what constitutes justice. We all know that certain actions are always wrong, while others are always right. It is always wrong, for instance, to take another's life. Stealing is clearly problematic, as well as lying. It is always appropriate to be compassionate. It is also right to be kind, loving, and merciful toward all, but especially to the vulnerable or suffering. If someone is under attack, we should come to their rescue.

Plato explored the nature of justice in endless detail in his massive dialogue *The Republic,* a utopian document, which was the first attempt in the West to reflect on the creation of a perfect society.[1] Plato demonstrates that understanding justice requires more than a philosophical discussion, that we can only understand the nature of justice in the context of an ideal state, the *polis,* where we can see it at work in the interactions of citizens.

But that best understanding is still very elusive. In the seventh book of *The Republic,* Plato developed his insights in terms of what we call the Allegory of the Cave.[2] He argued that what we know in this world is like a play of shadows on the wall of a subterranean cave. We don't know reality as it is; our ordinary experience affords us a view only of these shadows. In the cave, prisoners are chained so that they can look only straight in front of themselves. Behind their backs people are carrying all sorts of objects, while behind them a great fire rages. This fire casts shadows of the objects in front of the prisoners. The prisoners all think the shadowy images are real and thus give them a status they don't really possess.[3] One of the prisoners, a wise philosopher, breaks his chains, climbs out of the cave, and beholds the sun, or the Form of the Good — Plato's idea of God. The philosopher knows the objects on the cave's wall aren't real, and he returns to the cave to inform his fellow prisoners of the sun he's discovered.[4]

Plato's presentation is a brilliant metaphor of the human condition. What we think we know are mere figments, not substantial realities. If Plato is correct, society is incapable of knowing the true nature of justice, because it lacks the foundation for adequate knowledge. But Plato also realized something that few have emphasized since: If a compassionate order that is fair and sensitive to human needs is present in the social and political life of a people, then genuine justice can happen. Justice requires a just political order, as well as justice of the soul, in each one of us. Justice is the wise disposition of harmony in society and in all our relationships, as St. Augustine saw as well. Society's survival and well-being rest on the functions of rulers, warriors, merchants, and workers, whose ultimate welfare is in turn served by justice itself. Plato believed justice would only exist in a state, and to a more perfect degree if wise people ruled the state. He believed that only they have the ability to understand the nature and function of justice in the polis and in our lives.

The Role of Awareness

My own understanding of justice has been guided by my Christian faith. I've learned that justice does indeed require wisdom. It must be nourished by awareness; it doesn't just happen. This awareness, in my experience, allows us to look at others with loving kindness, mercy, and compassion. And, again, awareness is nurtured by mystical contemplation. I will discuss this idea at greater length in chapter 10.

Awareness takes us beyond self-interest, even beyond the focus on our families. Awareness fosters our understanding of the interconnectedness of all beings. It allows us to understand that justice simply cannot be defined or implemented without taking into account the interdependence of all beings. This very spiritual understanding fits well within Plato's classical notion of justice, since it required the state with its interconnected members and interests. The principle of interdependence means that the social totality, the whole of humankind, is equally responsible before society. And it implies equal rights for all the members of this totality, in which each of us has a place. Awareness forces us to see beyond our own good, and the good of our family and friends, to the greater good of the whole. This is the nature of justice: the awareness of the larger human and Divine Reality that surrounds us on every side.

As a Christian monk, I also view justice this way, but my faith adds some subtlety to the definition. Applying the Gospel to the sphere of justice, we see that it is really the existence of love or charity in the social, economic, political, and cultural domains. This charity, or selfless love, is immersed in and springs from the realization of the interconnectedness of us all. That is one of the implications of the Christian notion of the Mystical Body of Christ. We are all united in that Body. The Mystical Body is a way of speaking about our essential interdependence.

It is selfless love, *agape,* or in the tradition of the Catholic Church, *caritas,* that characterizes the true nature of justice. Love and compassion extend our capacity to see beyond the horizon of our individually oriented American and Western ideology of freedom. Justice can be actualized in our lives only if it reflects the larger reality of who we truly are — not isolated beings in a social, economic, political, and cultural conception of social Darwinism. A society based only on the survival of the fittest, in which capitalism reigns supreme, makes true justice impossible. Justice must rest on equality and fairness in the application of law and in the fair distribution of opportunities and resources.

We must become aware of justice's usually imperfect application. For example, nowhere is the great disparity between how the criminal justice system treats minorities more evident than in the application of capital punishment. Recent years have seen dozens of instances of innocent prisoners on death row, people railroaded by sloppy or fabricated evidence. The state of Illinois had fourteen well-known cases of innocent men released from death row in one year. This reveals a criminal justice system out of control, as well as a dual system: one for African Americans and one for whites.

Examples of injustice are everywhere. Women are often paid far less for the same work that men do. The rights of illegal aliens are disregarded by irresponsible employers who exploit them for paltry wages. This economic injustice against the faceless poor, mostly people from Latin America, is widespread. The immigrants frequently have no recourse, and they often live in deplorable conditions. These injustices, and countless others, are routinely tolerated by the business community, the police, and our elected officials.

The eye of contemplation cuts through the falsity of the system's convenient notions of justice; it sees to its heart, its hidden motives, and its transparent agendas. Being in the world with awareness, I strive for a healthy conscientization, to become sensitive to the issues of justice and social oppression, of racism and the plight of the homeless, the poor living on the margins of society. The Catholic Church has a long history of conscientization, of seeking an informed social conscience. And mystics with an awakened and enlightened conscience are capable of real leadership in spreading conscientization around the world. A wonderful example of a mystic with an awakened conscience was the Trappist monk Thomas Merton, who wrote with far-reaching effect on war, peace, racism, poverty, and the horrific nightmare of the Nazis.

Contemplative awareness has helped develop clarity in

conscience, and this clarity has become the source of my own work for justice, particularly in the areas of the Tibetan struggle, the homeless poor, the religions' role in working for peace, and ecological responsibility. Although these matters often feel overwhelming, I know I have a responsibility to do something. I can only view these problems through the Gospel. The Gospel, as an ethics of love, displaces the fragmented values of a hard and profane view of justice and shows us a vision of life in which justice, inspired by love, truly embraces the importance and preciousness of all sentient beings. The Gospel, in this divine, agapic ethics, turns the world and its selective values on its head. It is absolute in its conviction and uncompromising in its mission: to live in accordance with love in all relationships and to recognize that there is no higher priority than the vision of equality and well-being depicted in the Gospel. This vision has inspired all of my activism, but it has been especially inspiring of my continuing efforts on behalf of the Tibetan people.

THE WORK TO FREE TIBET

The Chinese invaded Tibet in 1949, incorporating this proud, noble nation into their regime. The Dalai Lama, his government, and his people made every effort to coexist with the Chinese authorities and colonists, but the Chinese kept turning the screw tighter and tighter until it became unbearable for the Tibetans. In March 1959 this intolerable oppression resulted in the people's uprising against their oppressors in an explosion of anger, resentment, and frustration. The Chinese military and police brutally put down the rebellion. The situation had deteriorated so badly that the Dalai Lama fled into exile in India with one hundred thousand of his people. He has been in India ever since, with the seat of his government in Dharamsala, in the Himalayan region of the subcontinent.

The Chinese have instituted in Tibet a systematic campaign to destroy Tibetan culture, which rests on Vajrayanja Buddhism, the "diamond tradition." They went on a rampage of destruction, devastating six thousand monasteries. Thousands of books, pieces of sacred art, and priceless cultural objects were destroyed. The Chinese imprisoned tens of thousands of Tibetans and engaged in regular torture to acquire information; they kept control through terror. Although they continue to torture Tibetans, in recent years they've done some window dressing for Westerners, rebuilding a few monasteries, giving the impression that things have returned to normal. They are also trying to erase any memory of the Dalai Lama in the hearts and minds of the people. To this end, they have made it a major offense for any Tibetan to possess a photo or image of the Dalai Lama. Of course many Tibetans ignore this prohibition and hide their photographs of His Holiness.

For as long as I have been involved with the Tibetans, I have been impassioned by their moral, nonviolent struggle with the People's Republic of China. I have known His Holiness the Dalai Lama since April 1988 when we first met at an official Catholic-Buddhist Monastic Dialogue. Since that time we have collaborated on a number of projects and over the years, we have become great friends. This relationship has led to wonderful friendships with many other Tibetans, including the Dalai Lama's younger brother, Tenzin Choegyal, his wife, Rinchen Khando, and their two children.

Looking into the eyes of the Tibetans I know and of so many others, I am aware of the great suffering they have endured since 1950, of the unbelievable injustice done to them, of the continuing acts of oppression they experience. It is not possible to interact with Tibetans and not discern their agony. When I began to perceive this suffering, it had a profound impact on me and has played a role in my evolving commitment to the Tibetan cause. Whenever I become discouraged at the slow pace of progress toward resolution, I remember the eyes of so many of my Tibetan brothers and sisters, all conveying the same message: We need your help in our struggle. I am also inspired by their supreme patience. I decided long ago that I would do everything in my power to assist the Tibetan people until they are finally free, their culture is secure, and their rights protected.

I try on every available occasion to make known to others the situation of the Tibetan people: through speaking, writing, interviews, and personal conversations. I instruct my students about the Tibetan cause. This is what it takes and it is something we can all do. Many who hear me speak or who talk with me pick up on my passion for this cause. My goal is to spark people's consciences by enlightening them about this tragedy.

The cause of Tibet is vital to our planet. It affects us all. I discern in the Tibet issue an important opportunity for the world to move toward greater cooperation, peace, and the transformation and enlightenment of the global ethos. Tibet represents a precious, endangered culture and faith, with a highly developed understanding of humankind's spiritual potential. Tibetan Buddhism offers a rare kind of wisdom, one the world desperately needs. Another reason to enter this struggle is simple: Tibet stands alone in her crisis. And no nation, other than the Czech Republic under the leadership of Václav Havel, has publicly acknowledged this intolerable oppression. Although considerable political support for His Holiness the Dalai Lama and his government-in-exile exists in the United States Congress, little has been done by any president to challenge Chinese leadership over their illegal and immoral forced occupation and oppression of Tibet. Indeed, the last several administrations have been far more focused on free trade with China than they have on China's egregious human rights violations.

I believe the world could learn much from direct involvement in the Tibetan cause. Its nonviolent character reinforces the value of a peaceful resolution to virulent conflicts, particularly ones that combine religion and statehood, like that between Jews and Arabs in the Middle East, Catholics and Protestants in Northern Ireland, or Hindus and Muslims on the subcontinent. We need vision in these areas of the world where ongoing disputes have yielded enormously tragic results. The planet cannot afford more wars, and nonviolence offers hope of graduating from reliance on the institution of war to the stable promise of global peace based on dialogue.

This transformation is not something that can happen easily; it takes a leap in our imaginative capacity even to envision it. History belongs to those who can name it, and this process is about naming the possibility of a catalyst whose activity could culminate not only in the freedom of the Tibetan nation but also in the empowerment of an integrated vision of the human family.

Awakening the Catholic Church

As a monk, as a contemplative mystic whose tradition is Catholicism, for which I feel a deep love, loyalty, and commitment, I have focused my attention and efforts primarily on conscientizing the Catholic Church. More precisely, I feel I can make the most difference by working on this particular angle in the Tibetan struggle. It has been and remains an uphill struggle to move this huge institution to realize it has a moral responsibility to speak out for and in support of the Tibetan people. The almost absolute silence of the Catholic leadership, from the pope down, about the sufferings of the Tibetan people has shocked me. It has caused me to temper my youthful idealism about the Church's nature and role as spokesperson for the oppressed and the poor.

Over many years I have tried many approaches to focusing Rome's attention on Tibet. I have presented the many reasons why the Catholic Church has a sacred obligation to champion the cause of the Tibetans, but Church officials have been adroit at circumventing the issue and any possible commitment. The Vatican's obvious desire to placate China, and thus avoid jeopardizing possible future concessions related to the Catholic Church in China, have caused their deafening silence. The Chinese government is unwilling to give Rome control over this large group of many millions, but Rome keeps hoping for a breakthrough. There are actually two Catholic Churches in China: the official church, called the Patriotic Association, partially controlled by the Chinese government, and the underground church, which refuses to do the PRC's bidding. Rome wishes to regain control over both these churches and unite them under its leadership.

Pope John Paul II certainly has the ability to make Tibet a global issue and priority. Just as he made Poland and the former Soviet empire his focus in the first half of his long pontificate, he could just as effectively concentrate on Tibet. His advocacy on behalf of the peoples of Eastern Europe and the Soviet Union aided the gradual unraveling of the Soviet bloc. This pope is clearly sympathetic to the sufferings of the Tibetans, but he has been unwilling to exert any leadership on behalf of Tibet's culture — or even to openly support human rights and religious freedom in Tibet. Nor has any Vatican official ever addressed the Tibetan matter.

At the 1993 Parliament of the World's Religions, a Catholic organization called Monastic Interreligious Dialogue (MID), of which I was a member, sponsored a Christian-Buddhist Monastic Dialogue, mentioned earlier. A year before this event, when Father Thomas Keating was the chairman of Monastic Interreligious Dialogue, he approved, along with the board of MID, an idea I presented, which was to formulate a document entitled "Resolution on Tibet." Here is the text of the original resolution, which I drafted with Sister Pascaline Coff and Father James Connor:

RESOLUTION ON TIBET

We have observed the intense suffering of the Tibetan people that has been inflicted on them for more than four decades. It is with concern, empathy, a deep sense of responsibility, and solidarity [with the Tibetan people] that we express our collective outrage at the brutal and callous actions of the People's Republic of China in Tibet. These actions include cultural genocide, torture, forced abortion, sterilization, and [the] systematic violation of the human rights of the Tibetan people, as well as deforestation and dumping of nuclear waste in Tibet. Above all, the massive transfer of Chinese immigrants into Tibet, which has already transformed the Tibetans into an insignificant minority in their own country, threatens the very existence of the Tibetan national and cultural identity. Such actions are thoroughly reprehensible and morally repugnant to all people within the religions, and even to those with no religion. Therefore, considering the seriousness of the situation in Tibet, we call for the complete and immediate restoration of the legitimate rights of the Tibetan people, and urge the international community to address the issue of Tibet at various forums, in particular at the United Nations.[5]

This statement presents the entire situation succinctly and urgently. Unfortunately, and predictably, it disturbed some Catholic officials, at least behind the scenes, and there were attempts to intimidate me into silence. These officials pressured the MID board to rescind the document and to push me off the board on a canonical pretext that I wasn't in a monastic community, a sneaky way to silence dissent on the Catholic Church's lack of leadership.

The MID board felt compelled to replace the resolution with another document, and they did, but it lacked the first draft's punch. It imitated the legal language of the United Nations and international treaties. There was no inspiration or clarity in the newer statement, and of course it fell on deaf ears. MID is clearly very supportive of the Tibetans, but one of the lay advisors with strong ties to Rome pushed the board in this direction. I continue in my attempts to raise the consciousness of the Catholic leadership about Tibet. In recent years some leaders have been willing to listen. Everyone in Rome acknowledges the profound concern of the Holy See, but then claims that little can be done at the moment, continuing the ongoing flight from concrete action.

Other Consciousness-Raising Efforts

Unfortunately, fear of Chinese reprisal runs deep, and the Catholic Church has not been the only institution to turn its back on Tibet's plight. I have also tried to advance the cause with the Parliament of the World's Religions, and indeed with the whole interfaith movement. Again and again I have broached the Tibetan cause with the board of the Parliament, on which I have served since 1993, and I have experienced continuing frustration trying to stir the consciences of my fellow directors.

When His Holiness the Dalai Lama recognized the reincarnation of the Panchen Lama some years ago, and China disputed his recognition with their own, I saw a good opportunity to challenge the Parliament to take a small and subtle political step for Tibet. I proposed that the Parliament write a letter to His Holiness congratulating him on the recognition of the Panchen Lama and expressing our great joy at this happy event. There were two disapproving voices, predictably a Catholic and an Orthodox member. When it came time to vote, 75 percent voted in favor of sending the letter, but behind our backs that night, the two dissenting members pressured the chairman of the Parliament not to send the letter, threatening to resign if he did. It was never sent.

Now with a new chairman who is unafraid of a challenge and the need for effective activism, the Parliament has taken a fresh approach. His commitment to this new direction was tested in August 2000 when the United Nations Summit of Religious and Spiritual Leaders Peace Conference was being readied. Outrageously, the Dalai Lama wasn't invited. The Parliament, as cosponsor of the event, sent a strongly worded letter to Kofi Annan, the secretary general of the U.N.

In concert with Richard Rosenkranz, a dear friend who orchestrated a campaign to inform the media of the injustice, Parliament board members wrote personal letters to the secretary general and joined in an extensive global petition, which gathered more than ten thousand signatures. Annan relented, and Bawa Jain, the secretary general of the conference, was forced to invite the Dalai Lama at the last minute. Of course His Holiness couldn't attend, but he sent a delegation. The event became a public relations disaster for the U.N. but a bonanza of public attention for the Tibetan cause. Both the Parliament and Rosenkranz reacted with dedicated vigor to the moral cowardice of the U.N., an organization that has never done anything for Tibet! Fear of China constrains this global body, and yet it seeks to be a moral arbitrator among the nations.

Rosenkranz has also founded an important new initiative called the Interfaith Call for Universal Religious Freedom and Human Rights. Since its founding in 1998 it has blossomed into a movement with hundreds of thousands of participants. The Call was a spin-off of World Tibet Day, which occurs every year around the time of the Dalai Lama's birthday, July 5. World Tibet Day, meant to draw the attention of the planet to the ongoing tragedy of the Tibetan people, was founded by Richard in 1998 with some very useful counsel from Tenzin Choegyal, His Holiness's younger brother and advisor. WTD is now being observed in more than fifty cities in twenty countries and urges the restoration of all basic freedoms for the Tibetan people: religious, cultural, and political.

By contrast the Interfaith Call does not mention political freedoms at all, but rather focuses solely on religious freedom and human rights; many major religious organizations, including the Catholic Church, are comfortable discussing religious freedom, and also to some extent human rights, but get very nervous when talk turns to political freedoms, even though many freedoms often labeled political — like freedom of speech — are obviously also basic human rights.

The response to the Interfaith Call has been impressive, and its work will continue until Tibet is finally free, or until there is a groundswell of support from the grassroots of the religions, especially the Catholic Church, forcing the leadership to take a stand. The situation requires a total commitment, like the stand taken by religious communities during the powerful years of the Civil Rights movement.

From the depths of my inner awareness of the Gospel, I

know that the Gospel's teaching of compassion and selfless love demands action of us. My absolute support of the Tibetans is closely tied to my commitment to the Gospel, which governs my decisions, attitudes, and actions. If I'm relentless about justice, it is because the Gospel compels me to be so. Though my advocacy of the Tibetan people clearly annoys the Church leadership, love demands this commitment of me.

PLURALISM AND PEACE

Pluralism is the position that all the religions together have equal value and an equal claim on the truth. Pluralism, I believe, is the key to transforming the religions from cultures of isolation and centers of potential conflict to dynamic communities that can work together. Through speaking, writing, teaching, and dialogue, I have been engaged in the work of building peace between and among the religions by promoting a spirit of genuine pluralism, which emphasizes the equality of all the traditions as well as the intrinsic right of each tradition to be. Only through a pluralistic approach can there be peace on earth. For far too long, the world's religions, through their narrow, exclusivist approach, have caused some of humankind's worst and most enduring conflicts. By setting aside their exclusivism, the religions can make peace with one another and be agents of peace all around the world. More precisely, the religions together hold the key to peace, not the nations, with their usual focus on militaristic power.

Acceptance of diversity as a fact and a cultural and existential constant is the primary goal of the interfaith movement. I don't think the world's religious and spiritual leaders realize how much influence and power to change the world they have if they work together, resisting the often irresponsible behavior of many political leaders. By making peace among themselves, they become examples for the rest of humanity. Working together they can have a substantial and lasting effect. The chief issue they must advance is peace, the central teaching of most traditions that tragically has been buried under their responsibility for so much conflict. One such step in that direction was the drafting of "The Universal Declaration on Nonviolence."

This particular document was conceived by the Dalai Lama and me in January 1989 during a long conversation at his residence in Dharamsala. The background of the declaration, and the desire to take this step, was the Iran-Iraq War, which was furiously raging at the time. We, and millions of others, were extremely alarmed at the facile way the belligerents used the Qur'an to support their cause, using religion to justify systematic violence and hatred of the worst kind. We felt the urgency to free religion from war making. The recent horrific abuses of the Qur'an have only made this disconnection more crucial.

The declaration itself, sponsored by His Holiness and MID under the leadership of Thomas Keating, is a kind of declaration of independence on the part of the religions from governments and groups advocating war. It stands as a monument in humankind's awareness of the importance of nonviolence for our future:

THE UNIVERSAL DECLARATION ON NONVIOLENCE

As members of religious groups throughout the world, we are increasingly aware of our responsibility to promote peace in our age and in the ages to come. Nevertheless, we recognize that in the history of the human family, people of various religions, acting officially in the name of their respective traditions, have either initiated or collaborated in organized and systematic violence or war. These actions have at times been directed against other religious traditions, groups, and nations, as well as within particular religious traditions. This pattern of behavior is totally inappropriate for spiritual persons and communities. Therefore, as members of world religions, we declare before the human family that:

Religion can no longer be an accomplice to war, to terrorism, or to any other forms of violence, organized or spontaneous, against any member of the human family. Because this family is one, global, and interrelated, our actions must be consistent with this identity. We recognize the right and duty of governments to defend the security of their people and to relieve those afflicted by exploitation and persecution. Nevertheless, we declare that religion must not permit itself to be used by any state, group, or organization for the purpose of supporting aggression for nationalistic gain. We have an obligation to promote a new vision of society, one in which war has no place in resolving disputes between and among states, organizations, and religions.

In making this declaration, we the signatories commit ourselves to this new vision. We call upon all members of our respective traditions to embrace this vision. We urge our members and all peoples to use every moral means to dissuade their governments from promoting war or terrorism. We strongly encourage the United Nations Organization to employ all available resources toward the development of peaceful methods of resolving conflicts among nations.

Our declaration is meant to promote such a new global society, one in which nonviolence is preeminent as a value in all human relations. We offer this vision of peace, mindful of the words of Pope Paul VI to the United Nations in October 1965: "No more war; war never again!"[6]

The declaration was signed and promulgated on April 2, 1991, in Santa Fe, New Mexico. Since its appearance, tens of thousands of people have signed it. It will be many years before its true meaning sinks in, or before the human family is ready to make such a commitment. This spirit of nonviolence and community, out of simple necessity in the face of terrorism and war, is growing in the interfaith movement and among religious traditions worldwide. We have reached a point in history where perhaps we can regard the importance of nonviolence as an ideal toward which we can all strive. This recognition has to dawn, as Martin Luther King Jr. so eloquently expressed it: "The choice is between nonviolence and nonexistence!"

CHAPTER 8

Tough Grace

A Contemplative Understanding of Suffering

Every person in the world knows the unpleasant reality of suffering; it is part of being human. Put more accurately, suffering exists for all sentient beings. Life, regardless of our many advantages, is always a struggle. We are often misunderstood, we face constant trials and setbacks, we deal with illness and poverty, we are frustrated in our work and our relationships. We endure bitter divorces, the death of loved ones, or illness and disease. Suffering in all its forms presents us with a strange enigma.

Our Western attitude toward life ill equips us to understand the nature and role of suffering. In the United States we exhibit compassion for the sick, yet few of us comprehend the role of illness in human development. Our civilization is so young, fixated on immature values and activities that distract us from the deeper meanings of human existence and of all sentient beings in the wheel of life. We often immerse ourselves in trivia as a way to avoid the more serious aspects of living. For Westerners, suffering, illness, and death are realities to be avoided and ignored, except when they strike our family or friends.

When I was growing up, my Uncle John often talked about illness and suffering, usually in the context of a difficult person we knew, someone who was self-centered, manipulative, insensitive, or uncaring. Uncle John's insight, born of deep faith, was that it might take a major sickness in this person's life to bring him to his senses and to open his heart. Calling it a kind of "tough grace," he saw suffering as a means for the Divine to reach us when we are unable to grow any other way. I like my uncle's explanation of suffering. As we shall see, a comprehensive understanding of suffering, one that considers both the highly developed viewpoints of Christianity and Buddhism, includes many other possible explanations as well.

Illness as a Journey to Wholeness

All my life I've been quite healthy. I've enjoyed a relatively robust vitality and have tried to strengthen it through a healthy diet, regular exercise, and meditation. Of course, my health is sometimes tempered by my busy schedule, lack of sleep, and many commitments. Nonetheless, it came as a total shock to me when I was diagnosed with palate cancer in November 2000. Nine days later I underwent a four-hour operation at Loyola Medical Center, where a surgeon removed half my palate, the upper left gum, teeth, and bone. It was such a loss, one I am still mourning. My surgeon was wonderful, as were the nurses and residents. After about five weeks of recuperation, I started a six-week process of radiation therapy. It was painful and difficult at times to eat, and my appetite dwindled. With this loss of appetite came a loss of weight as well.

From the moment of diagnosis, my friends surrounded me with love, care, and prayer. A number of women friends became my team, and they guided me every step of the way through the process of fighting the cancer and getting well again. Their nurturing made my recovery possible, and for that I will always be grateful. I also received a steady stream of loving visitors, mountains of mail, too many plants, and endless telephone calls. I was fortunate to have friends pick up the slack in my teaching, and I was able to get my grades in on time. I never realized I knew so many people. It was edifying, inspiring, and exhausting.

"There's a gift in this illness," many cancer survivor friends told me. "You don't see it yet, but you will." They were right. Many may wonder how suffering, especially an illness like cancer, can be a gift. This idea is certainly alien to a culture that rejects anything old, ugly, inconvenient, or uncomfortable. But within the context of a purposely spiritual life, suffering, and particularly illness, deepens our inner experience. Like spiritual practice and friendship, it very simply focuses our attention on what is really important — not on what passes away, but on those essential activities that carry us forward: prayer, meditation, surrender, humility, and loving compassion.

Perspective rises out of duality. If not for rain, we might never learn to love a sunny day. Suffering forces us to see beyond where we might be stuck. It helps us to transcend our attachments, our hidden agendas, our elaborate attempts to have it our own way. An illness like cancer, or any serious sickness, draws us to a subtler center of awareness, a center that reorders our values. It cuts away all the excess. It throws us into utter simplicity; we understand precisely what we really need. It invites us to see, to be aware, to change, to grow, to become what we are not yet but what we can be with commitment, effort, and discipline. It reveals to us our naked poverty and yet shows that in this poverty lies our hope of becoming who we really are: compassionate, loving beings.

My illness stripped me of everything; all things lost their immediate value or importance for me. I began to view things in a different light: the light of awareness. Making money, which has never been a real goal of mine, seemed even more unworthy of my attention. Ambition was even less significant. Honors and professional opportunities also seemed empty, devoid of any intrinsic value. All the activities people hold as dear I saw as useless and distracting. I saw too much talking as useless, ceaseless chatter and shied away from it. My old joys became meaningless in the light of my confrontation with my mortality.

At the time of my diagnosis, our country was in the throes of an inconclusive presidential election. I was passionately committed to the Democratic ticket. Yet, after the diagnosis, I lost all interest in the outcome. It wasn't so much that I no longer cared; rather, I saw the election in the larger light of life, death, and eternity. Lately, I've returned to my old interest in politics, though I see it differently, regarding it with a certain amount of tentativeness.

I realized I could die from this cancer. This sober realization cleared away all my other preoccupations. It was isolating. I felt I was in a glass cage, that no one could hear me. I felt alone with my fears, and they ate away at my peace. I had to struggle against my worries. Casting them down with prayer and determination, I began to learn to control them. And then the love of my friends helped to clear away the isolation. Part of my program for healing and recovery has been to deal squarely with my fear of mortality, to banish it from my mind and heart. This fear has a way of keeping you prisoner; it lessens your freedom.

Perhaps more than in any other part of life, in confronting fear, our spirituality demonstrates its precious value.

The Gift of Humility

Illness also deepens our humility. At first, cancer seems like a terrible humiliation, and to a certain degree it is. It is the most dramatic demonstration of our ultimate fragility and weakness. This gift of greater humility allows us to see ourselves as we are, freed from all our illusions. Humility cuts through our pretensions, our aspirations, our goals, and our attitudes toward others. Humility born of suffering, illness, and emotional turmoil serves our growth, inspiring us to make a change, to embrace a subtler form of psychological and spiritual well-being. This humility accelerates inner growth by traversing the darkness of spiritual trial and the shadow of death. It opens us up to receive the benefits of this darkness. Humility makes us available to God, and the humility of heart promoted by suffering and illness concentrates its power on our inner struggle to surrender to the Divine.

These many levels of humility of heart were well known in the monastic traditions of the West. St. Bernard of Clairvaux wrote a keenly aware treatise about them for his monks.[1] St. Benedict, the father of Western monasticism and the author of *The Rule of St. Benedict,* also wrote a great deal about this subject. Benedict drew on the desert tradition and the New Testament for his inspiration, demonstrating that humility is one of the pillars of monastic life.[2] Through humility we see the truth of our strengths and limitations, the unconscious roots of our weaknesses. Benedict, in his great wisdom, clearly saw the role of humility in the spiritual life.

In the evolution of humility during my illness, I noticed it calling me to greater acts of self-surrender and charity.

Benedict tells us that obedience is the first degree of humility, and I have realized that the Divine was, and is, demanding that I be obedient to the Spirit. Humility offers these insights with a clarity that defies reason. It is a clarity born of wisdom, another gift of the Spirit.

My illness also revealed to me how reliant on God and others we become in times of extreme vulnerability. Becoming dependent on others, and certainly on God, showed me how illusory my conviction of innate autonomy was. Autonomy is never absolute; it operates within the narrow perimeters of wellness and youth. It is very fragile, and yet we cling to it as if it's the most treasured object in our life's history. Although a measure of autonomy is psychologically healthy, it also becomes a way to separate ourselves from people, to think that we are somehow better than others because we are autonomous and don't need them. Bede Griffiths often remarked in conversations, homilies, and prayer that "sin is separation." Sin is living as if we were separate and better, isolating ourselves from our brothers and sisters and from all other sentient beings. Suffering, particularly illness, knocks a hole in this insidious attitude and drives home our interdependence. Illness frees us from the isolation that this illusory autonomy and separation impose and opens us to spiritual and psychological growth.

The Gift of Divine Union

Before I started radiation therapy, Thomas Keating came to Chicago to give a weekend retreat to the Spiritual Life Task Circle, a group belonging to and mandated by the Parliament of the World's Religions. Thomas and I had talked about my illness weeks before the retreat and during it. Since my early twenties, he has guided me on my spiritual journey. Thomas told me that he was convinced that my bout with cancer was a dark night of the soul, an inner purification preceding a permanent union with the Divine. He told me that my illness was a step forward, a sign of real progress.

As I reflected on this insight, I began to see the truth of his words. This dark night of the soul has concentrated my attention on what is really necessary. I began letting go of everything, since everything seemed so meaningless in relationship to the goal: union with God. The inner darkness of my spirit was inviting me to subtler levels of surrender. I found myself wanting to radiate the intense love of the Divine Presence, and that became my purpose during my recuperation. As I was lying on the gurney, waiting for each treatment, I would visualize the radiation coming in and being transmuted by my love into beams of loving compassion toward all. This image carried my intention and effectively galvanized my love.

The dark night of the soul brought about by this illness also provided me with deeper self-knowledge, or I should say, reminded me of what I already knew about myself. I saw that I was struggling with God's will for me. I had been resisting total surrender, holding back part of my commitment. The cancer forced me to reexamine my hidden motives, my unspoken assumptions about happiness, for example, that I could have happiness on my own terms, that I could be happy regardless of others rather than in relation to others. Perhaps I wouldn't have gone through this process of self-examination if it hadn't been for the sickness, or perhaps this process would have been greatly delayed.

I feel that I've gained from my illness the great gift of spiritual grace, a permanent acquisition that I must now build on. The direction is clear to me, as is the effort required. In a sense, my bout with cancer has been like a long retreat for me. Retreats should help us take stock of our lives, rectify our course, and set a new direction. I now feel I am ready for some great breakthroughs on my spiritual journey.

OPENING THE WISDOM EYE

As illness opens the heart to growth in relation to the Divine, it also awakens the "wisdom eye" from its slumbers. The wisdom eye is essentially a subtle capacity to see, to know, to understand, and to respond. Classically the wisdom eye is activated through mystical experience or intense spiritual practice. Sometimes the process happens spontaneously while we are engaged in some simple activity, like washing dishes, raking leaves, doing laundry, painting, or listening to music. In fact, anything can stimulate the opening of the wisdom eye, and the Zen tradition, with its experience of *satori*, or seeing into one's own nature, also called *kensho*, has devoted much attention to this topic.

Suffering, and particularly an illness like cancer, can activate this contemplative capacity in us. Although I like to think my wisdom eye was opened long before my illness appeared, through many years of contemplation, the suffering I experienced through the illness deepened this capacity. The shock of my diagnosis propelled my attention — or focused it more intensely — on realities beyond my normal perception and uncovered for me what was important here and now, like being present to others, being fully engaged in my activities, and appreciating my friends and loved ones.

Even before my diagnosis, in fact the very night before, I had three powerful experiences: a dream, a unitive experience, and the perception of nonhuman presences. As I mentioned earlier, during the years since his death, my Uncle John has regularly shown up in my dreams. This dream was very disturbing. Uncle John's body was floating in the ocean, although he wasn't dead. A strong feeling of danger pervaded the dream, as if warning me of impending crisis. Then, as I lay awake in bed the next morning, I experienced a full and comprehensive encounter with God, in which the Spirit took hold of my entire being and poured love into me, saturating my being. This experience was all-encompassing. The Divine communicated its love to me intimately, enveloping me totally. Then just as quickly as the Spirit came it went, but what preceded its departure was a strange meeting and conversing of presences in my bedroom. They were talking about something that I couldn't make out, and though the presences were vague in form, they were clearly there in the room.

Each event is an example of the wisdom eye, or the eye of contemplative understanding, at work. I believe that together these instances were a harbinger meant to prepare me for my diagnosis and also, perhaps, to put my mind at ease about the eventual outcome. Each in its own way was part of a special grace and taken together they were a gift to support me in this period of trial. I know that these phenomena are supernatural in origin and intention. My wisdom eye, my contemplative capacity, was on to the truth before I had even learned of the diagnosis.

The wisdom eye has many levels: cosmological, metaphysical, psychological, mystical, moral, and spiritual. Though these dimensions are always present and accessible, they may be heightened through suffering. Direct knowledge of ultimate principles, not just speculation about them, represents the cosmological and metaphysical dimensions. These ultimate principles are insights into the nature, origin, and purpose of the universe and the ground out of which it has emerged into being. The metaphysical level of the wisdom eye's scope of perception allows us to understand reality as it actually is, unadorned by our distortions and misperceptions. The psychological and mystical levels include a deep perception of the interconnectedness of all sentient beings. The moral reality shows itself in an innate sense of solidarity with all those who suffer. The moral and spiritual aspects of the contemplative capacity often express themselves in a desire to remove suffering from others, or if this is not possible, to at least not add to what others have to carry. We have so eloquently witnessed the great corporal works of mercy, as the Catholic tradition calls them, in the life and activities of the great saints, the social gospel of Christianity, socially engaged Buddhism and Hinduism, and selfless service to the homeless poor. These all reflect the moral and spiritual dimensions of the wisdom eye.

The response of compassion to great pain and suffering all around us is born from a deep ground of love, that ground on which we all must stand as we cultivate our spiritual lives. This is the vivifying source of our solidarity with all beings, the energy out of which we respond to all those in need, especially those needing to be consoled and understood. Suffering and illness clear away the self-centeredness to which our culture habituates us and establishes us profoundly in that ground of love that is the Divine, the source of all good. We are given the perspective to grasp our true situation in life and to understand the nature of the reality in which, according to the Acts of the Apostles, "we live, and move, and have our being."[3]

TOUGH GRACE

Like the notion of tough love, in which families and friends must help their loved ones escape destructive patterns by challenging them, tough grace is a gift from God to the soul in need of growth. Tough grace is the Divine's way of reaching certain souls who may need a measure of suffering to rise above their preoccupations, or to take others deeper into His love. Tough grace is first and foremost a form of divine communication. It operates through illness, injustice, psychological problems, and misunderstandings to bring us to a single-minded attention on what is important for our ultimate development.

Tough grace is never about punishment. God doesn't punish us with suffering. Nor is it a means of divine coercion. The Spirit just doesn't work that way. The Divine is not wrathful, as the biblical tradition sometimes represents it. This wrathfulness is not in God, but in the human misinterpretation of God's words and actions. Suffering provides us with lessons that dispose us more readily to divine union and helps us to consider those things we often take for granted. Tough grace puts these things in front of our face. We are pushed to make decisions about our relationship with God. Tough grace brings about a radical simplification of our lives by first purifying our hidden motives with love and compassion. It highlights just what we need for the spiritual journey and counsels us to leave the rest behind. In this way, tough grace is itself a gift, though it may be the kind of gift we aren't too anxious to receive, until we witness its profound transformative effects on us. Then we understand.

An incident from the life of St. Teresa of Avila, the sixteenth-century Spanish Carmelite mystic, speaks to the divine intention behind tough grace. Teresa was journeying by horse-drawn carriage in the pouring rain, far from any town, when one of the carriage wheels got caught in the mud. After the passengers had climbed out of the carriage, she stood in the rain while the driver was trying to fix the wheel. Disheartened, she spoke to God: "Why do you treat me this way, Lord?" God responded: "Teresa, my beloved child, this is how I treat all my friends!"

Not wanting God to have the last word, she remarked: "No wonder you have so few friends!"

Teresa bore many trials in her day, most related to the reform of the Carmelite Order. She and John of the Cross were attacked by members who resisted reform, and John was imprisoned by his own friars. In fact, it was from his cell that he wrote some of his great mystical works. Of course, saints and mystics necessarily share in the sufferings of humanity, but also in the Spirit's sufferings. We all share in these sufferings, according to our capacity, acceptance, and generosity. From the Christian perspective, this should not surprise us. God the Father required that his own son, Jesus, suffer horrifically and saw to it that his agony would be potentially redemptive for all humankind. Christ's Passion represents the most severe form of tough grace. Central to the Christian mystery is that the Beloved Son, the one the Divine Father loved from eternity, was asked to make this greatest sacrifice, his own life, as an act of redemptive love for us. Tough grace required that the Son of God suffer far more than most human beings could endure.

If the Father asks his own son to embrace the worst kind of suffering, even if briefly, can we who claim to be his friends expect anything less? What should be clear is that suffering is not all negative in its implications. Suffering stretches us and stimulates our growth. Through tough grace, the Divine draws out of us some of the greatest miracles of inner change.

THE BUDDHA'S VIEW

The Buddha realized, and stated in his first Noble Truth, that suffering is fundamentally part of life: the suffering of birth, illness, old age, and death itself. I think everyone would agree with the Buddha's contention that suffering is natural to this existence. The Buddha identifies another kind of suffering that is essentially self-inflicted. Self-inflicted suffering is caused by our own selfish desires, our stubborn attachments, our craving to have things our way. Most moral evil in the world is caused by this kind of desire. Sobering examples are the brutal regimes of Hitler, Pol Pot, Stalin, and Mao; their possession and use of power led to great human suffering.

The Buddha understood how this self-inflicted suffering was, at least partially, under our control. We can eliminate the suffering caused by the afflictive emotions like hatred, greed, and aversion by disengaging from our desires. To take the path of eliminating the roots of desires that cause suffering is the way of enlightenment. We cannot do anything to eliminate fundamental suffering, but we can do much to free ourselves from the self-inflicted sort, an essential part of being a Buddhist.

The Buddhist notion of *dukkha,* the term employed for suffering, is subtler than the English word *suffering. Dukkha* also connotes dread, anxiety, desperation, depression, rage, the basic unsatisfactory nature of life. *Dukkha* colors life with a depressive screen, a screen we ourselves create, sustain, and often complicate with our selfish schemes. We have (only!) to forgo our cravings, through spiritual practice and what the Buddha identified as the Eightfold Path. This well-known path includes ethical principles, like right view, right speech, right livelihood, right effort, and meditation concentration expressed in practice.

CHRIST'S VIEW

Jesus would have agreed with the Buddha's ideas about the two types of suffering. But he might have added the divine, salvific economy of suffering and grace. Jesus, in the Incarnation, performed a kind of divine composting. He took our sin, negativity, and inhumanity and transformed them by his sacrificial love, just as compost is slowly converted to rich earth. Jesus did not flee this agony but embraced it head-on. And according to the Christian tradition, through that act a cosmic, mystical transformation occurred.

This insight appears in some form in the lives of all the saints. The vast majority of saints never wished to be separated from their sufferings; they knew that their suffering was directly related to the Divine's sufferings, particularly as expressed in Christ's Incarnation and the Redemption. The saints desired to remain part of the divine, salvific economy of suffering; they wanted to participate directly and permanently in it, because they knew they were also sharing in the transformation of humankind's pain, agony, illness, inhumanity, injustice, cruelty, and indifference. The saints knew they had to participate in the inner agony to attain the final glory. This is similar to the Buddhist notion that we should never turn away from the sufferings of others.

SUFFERING AS REDEMPTION

In my life and spiritual development, and through my struggle with cancer, I have come to a new understanding of the nature of suffering. The insight that suffering has a redemptive quality strikes me deeply. I am convinced that suffering, when rightly understood and embraced generously, is ultimately a path to spiritual and moral, even psychological, transformation. This transformation is essentially what our spiritual journey is all about. Suffering is a bit of unpleasant assistance on the way. It helps us in the long run as we awaken to the ultimate goal of intimacy with the Divine, with boundless consciousness.

Each of us must face the reality of suffering in our own

lives and in the lives of our loved ones. None of us can escape illness, old age, and death. We must strive to understand this aspect of life and to find a way to integrate it into our experience. We are challenged to look more deeply into the meaning and reality of illness and suffering in human life and in all sentient beings. Like Tibetan lamas, who in their training are familiarized with dead bodies, driving home death's ultimate reality, we must face death straight on. Most of all, we have a responsibility to confront suffering, for it has much to teach us.

What are suffering and illness trying to teach us? We require a mature approach to this part of our lives, an approach that will allow us to understand the gift in the challenge, the jewel in the pain, the light in the darkness beyond the suffering. The progress of each one of us, as that of the human race itself, depends on a more adequate understanding of this mysterious reality in our lives.

For too long Western cultures have interpreted suffering and illness simply, and profanely, as tragedies with little or no meaning. Suffering, illness, and the various other challenges, are cut off from their ontological and spiritual roots. The Christian vision restores these roots.

Christ is said to have taken on himself the sufferings of humanity and the consequences flowing from them. More than that, suffering manifests an ultimately beneficial, salvific power that transforms all of human negativity into something beautiful, powerful, life-giving, and productive of positive results for everyone, at least potentially.

We are at a crossroads in how we understand pain, illness, and suffering. The human family is restless over the old approaches, because we know there is something more. It is our task now to understand this dimension of human experience in a new light, to free it from its useless context of secular meaninglessness. We possess the tools to gain insight, but we must look in the right direction. Sooner or later, each one of us must confront our own suffering. Then the question becomes what we will do with it. How will we regard it so that it enhances our well-being? Our task as humans is the same: wise understanding, so that we can make those decisions that will contribute to our eventual spiritual transformation through the mystery of our suffering.

Interspirituality

The Mystical Thread of a Monk in the World

As the barriers separating the religions and cultures of the world are collapsing, a new model is emerging, an intermystical, interspiritual paradigm that permits people from various traditions, or from no tradition, to explore the spiritual dimensions of any religion. More and more people find themselves rooted in one tradition while seriously investigating another.

While the great religions, in their respective beliefs and practices, have been isolated from one another, at their core they share a deeper dimension. This is the common ground that interspirituality explores: the dimension of mysticism across traditions. Interspirituality is based on the existential, innate interdependence of all beings, the essential interconnectedness of all reality. As do all sentient beings, the religions have a profound inner connection with one another and, ultimately, depend on one another for survival.

As the collapse of barriers has accelerated in recent years, we have witnessed what futurist Linda Grof calls a boundary meltdown. Boundary meltdown doesn't mean the loss of identity among the traditions but rather the freedom to experiment in our search for a spiritual path. It means that religions are no longer cultures set apart, but open systems conversing with the world and with one another either directly or through the agency of the interfaith movement.

Since 1977, as I have become more interested in the East, I have lived in this movement and embraced the phenomenon of free access across the traditions. This work has become second nature to me, a vital focus of my ongoing work and a labor of love. Interspirituality encompasses many traditions and projects, ranging from the spread of Eastern meditation practices among Christians, Jews, and Sufis; to interspiritual centers, such as the Osage Monastery, a monastic community dedicated to bringing Christianity, Hinduism, and Buddhism together; to the Christian-Hindu ashram Shantivanam; to Baptist churches that accept people of different traditions; to Christian *sannyasis* living as contemplative hermits in Arizona; to Christian *roshis* who combine Zen mastery with the teachings of Christ. Endless examples, with endless combinations of traditions, abound. And many extraordinary visionaries, such as Thomas Merton, Abhishiktananda, Rabbi Zalman Schacter-Shalomi, Ammachi, and Thich Nhat Hanh — all of whom I will touch on here — have done much to champion the cause of understanding among religious traditions. (For even more about these visionaries, see my last book, *The Mystic Heart.*) These men and women serve as shining examples to us all.

AN INTERSPIRITUAL VISION

Interspirituality presupposes an integral view of spirituality, first as an ideal and then as an actuality. Since the mystical is their common ground, all spiritualities share an integral possibility. In interspirituality, varied insights scattered like so many precious seeds among the religions are viewed as belonging to the inclusive domain of the mystical. Although most spiritual traditions have developed in isolation, they are all fundamentally part of the human depth. All forms of spirituality share this depth, though they conceive their goals and practices differently. The different forms of spirituality complement one another and complete the picture of what is required on the spiritual path.

Interspirituality rests on a vast community of insight and experience available to humanity at all times and in all places. This community embraces the collective wisdom of the human family. Behind this vast community of collective awareness is the one Spirit, inspiring breakthroughs to its realm, opening minds and hearts, transforming attitudes and wills, and encouraging growth in compassion, love, kindness, mercy, and sensitivity. Interspirituality includes the courageous tendency to religious and spiritual creativity, which springs from understanding how much can be gained by venturing out of one's comfort and familiarity and into other traditions. In a sense, to pursue an intermystical spiritual life is to be a real pioneer of the Spirit. It is not an easy path to travel, because not many maps exist yet, and many people fear losing their way, but it yields rich deposits of wisdom along the way. If we trust, keep moving on, and share our experience with others, while seeking their advice, we will be fine. In fact, uncertainty can lead to even greater spiritual realizations. Without the familiar rituals and beliefs of our tradition to fall back on, we sometimes come closer to realizing the true goals of religion.

Interspirituality is not an attempt to force synthesis where it is not possible. As the popular joke goes, What do you get when you cross a Unitarian with a Jehovah's Witness? Someone who knocks on doors for no particular reason! Although this may not be the most natural partnership, certainly the members of these traditions have much to teach one another. Forced synthesis won't work; practitioners approaching one another with open minds will. Let's look at some examples that convey the meaning of interspirituality. One fairly new form of spirituality is inspired primarily from the Christian tradition but has hold of something universal, something found in one form or another in all the great world's religions. The text for *A Course in Miracles* was written in the mid-seventies by two professors of medical psychology at Columbia University, Helen Schucman and William Thetford.[1] More precisely, Helen Schucman received the messages from the voice of the Spirit, and she wrote them down in shorthand, and William Thetford typed each message up the next day.

The Course, under the sponsorship of the Foundation for Inner Peace, proposes an approach to life and spirituality that emphasizes love over fear, trust over suspicion, knowledge over subjective perception or projection, integration over dualism, God over ego, holiness over self-centeredness, awakening over limitation, and salvation over keeping a closed heart. *The Course* proposes a way of coming into the fullness of salvation and enlightenment by choosing to live from the courage of love rather than from the temptation to fear. This inspired — in the true sense of the word — book has uncovered a universal principle of spiritual life.

The rapid and continuing spread of Eastern meditation practice among Jews, Christians, and even Muslims is another growing example of interspirituality. More and more people of varied faiths see some form of discursive or nondiscursive meditation as an essential part of spiritual practice. Discursive meditation emphasizes thought, insight, and sometimes even reflection — like Vipassana meditation of Theravada Buddhism. Nondiscursive meditation stresses the transcendence of thought, sensations, feelings, and especially of the ego and its hold on consciousness. Examples include various forms of Hindu, Buddhist, and Sufi meditation, as well as Centering Prayer and the Christian Meditation of John Main, an English Benedictine monk.

Meditation unites people of all faiths beyond words, doctrines, beliefs, and rituals. Hindus, Jews, Christians, Buddhists, Muslims, Unitarians, Sikhs, Jains, Native Americans, Quakers, and Taoists can all sit quietly together in meditation and have a deep experience of communion with one another and with Ultimate Reality. Most cities have meditation groups from various traditions meeting weekly. Often these meetings take place in church halls, synagogues, temples, and in members' homes. Meditation has become a permanent part of third-millennium mysticism. It has stood the test of time and is now achieving a universal presence in planetary culture. I think it's safe to predict that a century from now, meditation will be an integral part of every culture and spirituality.

Another example of interspirituality is the evangelical movement Jews for Jesus, which has been around for decades. These Jews, who have discovered Christ in the Christian sense, have also decided to remain Jews spiritually and culturally. Rather than giving up their Jewish identity, they seek to wed it to their Christian faith. They are full Jews in faith and ethnicity, but they view their Jewish faith as having a direct relationship with the Gospel. They essentially see Judaism and Christianity as two branches of the same faith at different stages of development. Although this group is small, consisting perhaps of as few as ten thousand members around the world, it has insight and direction that points the way for these two major world religions to forge a new relationship.

Interspiritual movements often cause problems for conservative members of faiths who are firmly entrenched in their traditions. They also raise all sorts of questions of identity. Many Israelis look on the Jews for Jesus movement with suspicion because it seems to threaten the Jewish faith through its attempts at conversion. It complicates further the question of what constitutes Judaism. Is it faith, culture, or ethnicity that defines Jewishness? These are difficult and challenging matters, and many would rather not have them thrust in their awareness by what they see as "fringe" groups.

Interspiritual Sites

Many efforts at interspiritual synthesis come in the form of meeting places where people of different traditions can come together to practice. One of the most fascinating, and eclectic, sacred spaces is Osage Monastery in Sand Springs, Oklahoma, which is dedicated to a profoundly interspiritual vision of life, more precisely, a Hindu-Christian and Buddhist-Christian vision. Named after the Osage tribe, and sited spectacularly in their territory, the monastery is a wonderful set of hermitages, with a community of nuns in the Benedictine tradition. Its founder, Sister Pascaline Coff, had roots in India with Father Bede Griffiths, and Osage was consecrated to bringing together Hinduism, Christianity, and Buddhism in contemplative practice. It is open to the world, welcoming people from all traditions.[2]

Another such contemplative community is "Friends of God" Dominican Ashram, founded in 1999 in Kenosha, Wisconsin, by a small group of Dominican friars. Dominican friars are not monks but mendicants, members of a Catholic religious order who don't own anything and work for a living. Officially called the Order of Preachers, or Dominicans, they were founded by St. Dominic in the early thirteenth century. The Dominican Ashram adds their own cross-tradition flavor to the order's goal of sharing the fruits of Christian contemplation with others.[3]

Of course, my favorite example of an interspiritual center is Shantivanam Ashram, the monastic community of Father Bede Griffiths, where he presided from 1968 to 1993. Shantivanam is Hindu in culture and Christian in faith but is completely given over to the reconciliation of Hinduism, Buddhism, and Christianity. At Shantivanam, the pillars hold up this unique community are found in meditation practice. Shantivanam has been consciously committed to interspirituality since its founding in 1950 by two French priests, Henri Le Saux, who later became Abhishiktananda, and Jules Monchanin. Both were Christians, but they both also donned the saffron *dhoti* and shawl of the Hindu *sannyasi*. In 1950, they were already exploring the depths of Hindu mysticism and renunciation previously uncharted by Christianity.

Under Bede Griffiths, this inculturation process has continued, and Bede has also introduced reading Buddhist, Taoist, Jewish, and Islamic sacred texts during common prayer along with Christian and Hindu ones. Long before it became a Christian-Hindu ashram, Shantivanam was sacred to *sadhus, sannyasis,* and *yogis*. It is a holy place, an oasis of peace containing special energies and graces, where miracles happen as a matter of course. Shantivanam has always had, for me, a magical quality, and countless souls have had intense mystical experiences there, including myself. For thousands of years it has been steeped in sacred practice, or *sadhana,* of mystical contemplation, and the austerities of ascetic saints. Shantivanam has become a profound example of interspiritual wisdom, a nexus for insight, experience, and mystical processes to come together. It facilitates mystical awareness across traditions, in an atmosphere of freedom and acceptance. It is a very precious place.

In a very different part of the world is the Church of Conscious Harmony in Austin, Texas, another interspiritual institution with ties to India. Founded several years ago by a remarkable couple, ministers Tim and Barbara Cook, the Church of Conscious Harmony has always been an interspiritual church in practice. What makes this community so unique is that it is a contemplative fellowship. In addition to regular Christian observance, members meditate twice a day. The leaders of the church have spent long periods in India; they seriously appreciate the culture and spirituality of the Indian tradition, and this appreciation is part of the church's self-understanding. This church spans the East and the West, even reaching to the Native Americans. Very few other communities of faith have this quality of openness to other traditions.

Then there are two extraordinary Carmelite priests who for more than twenty-five years have been living as hermits in the desert of Arizona. (To protect their solitude, I will not mention their names or their precise location.) The Carmelite Order follows a contemplative form of life, and these two friars discovered Abhishiktananda, his unique way of life in India, and his mystical writings. They decided to follow his vision of the spiritual life as Christian *sannyasis* in the desert of the Southwest. Theirs is a mystical path in the hiddenness of the wilderness that combines the interiority of India with the contemplation of Christian mystics. These hermits are following a hybrid, intermystical spirituality. They are unique pioneers on the frontiers of consciousness.

Perhaps more striking than these many other examples —
in the sheer integration of seemingly disparate faiths — are
the countless Christian *roshis* both in America and Europe.
With utter loyalty to their Christian faith and identity, these
meditation masters have adopted Zen as an expression of their
spiritual path, the central focus of their inner journey to
enlightenment, transcendence, and the Divine Reality. These
teachers, who have been recognized by the leaders of the Zen
schools in Japan, include the Reverend Robert Kennedy, a Jesuit
in New York City, the Reverend Susan Postal, an Anglican priest
also in the New York area, Dr. Ruben Habito, a professor at
Southern Methodist University in Texas, and Father Willigis
Jaeger, a Benedictine in Germany. These are only a few figures
in a large and growing interspiritual movement that is increasingly allowed and even accredited by two very different religious institutions, Zen Buddhism and Catholicism — though
perhaps it causes some concern in Rome!

INTERSPIRITUAL VISIONARIES

Thomas Merton

Long before the present preoccupation with the interreligious
encounter, the Trappist monk Thomas Merton was working to
open this door for the Catholic Church and American culture,
all from the Gethsemani monastery in Kentucky. For ten years
before his fateful trip to Asia in the fall of 1968, Thomas
Merton assimilated the major spiritual classics of the East into
his Christian understanding, particularly Zen Buddhist, Hindu
Vedanta, Yoga texts, and Taoist classics. Although Merton had
absorbed his own Catholic contemplative tradition very deeply,
he was consciously trying to relate the mystical insights of
other traditions with his own Christian faith.

Merton's instincts inclined him toward the openness of all

the traditions in a new relationship of solidarity, mutual trust, respect, honor, and learning. His work set an example to other seekers looking for the integration of a universal wisdom tradition. Although Merton did not live to see where his vision would lead, I believe he would be delighted by the intermystical character of our present course.

Abhishiktananda

Henri Le Saux, who became Abhishiktananda, or the "Bliss of the Anointed One," or "Bliss of Christ," was another monastic trailblazer. Little known in America, but celebrated in his native France and his adopted home of India, this lonely, even agonized figure accomplished something profoundly original at the dawn of the interspiritual age. He was at once a Catholic priest, a Christian contemplative, and a Hindu mystic, a pure *advaitin.* He left the security of his Benedictine monastery in Brittany for the wild vulnerability of the wandering *sannyasi.* The great modern Indian saint Ramana Maharshi awakened Abhishiktananda to the authenticity of Hindu mysticism, the radical nature of pure nonduality or *advaita.* Through months of meditation in the sacred caves of the holy mountain Arunachala, above Ramana's community in Tamil Nadu, India, he was drawn into a vortex of advaitic awareness that never left him. His advaitic experience overwhelmed him and became the mystical consciousness of his life.[4]

What he achieved was enormous. He pointed a way for Westerners to explore and relate to the mystical tradition of India, a way marked by the ultimacy of experiential awareness. In a sense, Abhishiktananda sacrificed himself for all those who would come after, for what he achieved was at the price of his past Catholic security. He had to push on, so seized was he by the reality of the Divine; there was no turning back for him.

Abhishiktananda's experience demonstrates the deep reality of the interspiritual quest. He knew in the depths of his interiority, as much as in the heights of his intellect, of the utter authenticity of the advaitic consciousness, an ultimate degree of awareness. His task was to reconcile this experience with his equally certain Christian mystical experience of contemplative consciousness — the inner reality of the Trinitarian mystery at the center of the Godhead. Anyone on the intermystical journey will gain much from reading and pondering Abhishiktananda's very rich inner life.

Bede Griffiths

Of course, my favorite interspiritual figure is Bede Griffiths, who, besides having a profound impact on my spiritual life, influenced the spiritual path of Europe, Australia, Canada, and more recently the United States. Bede delved into the deep ocean of Asian wisdom, assimilating insights through his reading in England long before his move to India in 1955. Father Bede in a sense domesticated his observance of renunciation, of *sannyasa,* by settling down in the ashram at Shantivanam, which he inherited from Abhishiktananda in 1968. Before Bede's tenure the ashram had been terribly neglected because Abhishiktananda was rarely around, preferring to spend long periods in his Himalayan hermitage in Uttarkashi.

Under Bede, Shantivanam bloomed, becoming a renowned interspiritual center. Part of the draw was, of course, Bede himself, the gentle, grandfatherly Englishman whose warmth, love, and learning attracted thousands each year to his gate. Bede's intermystical vision, his deeply synthetic ability, easily accommodated the Christian, Hindu, Buddhist, Sufi, Taoist, and Jewish traditions.[5] Bede had integrated a regular teaching on the interrelationship of these traditions' mystical core. Inspired by Bede's leadership as a spiritual master, Shantivanam became a special center devoted to the subtle, universal tradition undergirding the great world religions. All that Shantivanam has become is a result of Father Bede's incomparable leadership in creating an interspiritual nexus with charm, magic, and challenge.

Ammachi

Ammachi, or Amma, as she is affectionately called, is an extraordinary woman who by her presence and witness is contributing to an interspiritual culture around the planet. Everywhere Amma is celebrated as "the saint who hugs people." Often her teaching is simply the spirit exchanged in two people hugging. She will walk into a crowded room with two thousand people and won't leave until she has hugged every person! Her teaching is unconditional love, which she expresses in herself and how she treats everyone. A simple action such as hugging another can carry with it a priceless message of acceptance and healing. She has to be seen as an interspiritual mystic because of her support of Christians and Jews and her universal appeal, all from within her Hindu tradition.

Amma has also a reputation as a healer, and in India she has established hospitals, clinics, and centers for the poor. Her example of love reminds us of Mother Teresa, but unlike Mother Teresa, who lacked the interspiritual vision, Amma seems to embody interspiritual acceptance. By her emphasis on selfless service and charity, Amma will, I believe, hugely influence the future world.[6]

Raimon Panikkar

Raimon Panikkar in his very ancestry represents the marriage of East and West. His father was a Brahmin from Kerela in

South India and his mother was a Catholic from Barcelona, Spain. With doctorates in chemistry, philosophy, and theology, he has the background to seek integration. Panikkar's unique contribution to the interspiritual age comes in a profound understanding of the interrelationship of all the great world's religions. He considers himself equally Catholic, Hindu, and Buddhist. In one stroke he has bridged three traditions in a time when the fundamentalists criticize those who even study another traditions. Panikkar's brilliance, openness, and commitment to break down the barriers that have artificially separated the various religious communities for thousands of years have found their most effective voice in speaking and writing, in the great subtlety of his wisdom.[7] I believe, through his contribution to cross-cultural studies, and therefore, interspiritual wisdom, he is one of the most original thinkers of our time, advancing an intermystical understanding of the community of religions.

Brother David Steindl-Rast

Another interspiritual visionary is Benedictine monk Brother David Steindl-Rast. At the forefront of the interreligious movement that began in the 1960s, Brother David worked with figures like yogi Swami Satchidananda, New York Hasidic teacher Rabbi Gelberman, sufi master Pir Vilayat Khan, and Zen teacher Eido Tai Shi Mano in a collaborative movement for peace and justice among religious and spiritual leaders, and away from fundamentalism and the exclusivism it entails.

In awakening people to the new reality of acceptance, Brother David has always drawn on his eloquence as a speaker. I remember hearing him speak for the first time in 1971. He asked people to present their questions, one after another, *before* his talk. He proceeded to answer every one of them — about forty

— in the course of his lecture, not missing one! Brother David has done so much to open the hearts and minds of people to this age of communion among members of the world's spiritual traditions.

Thich Nhat Hanh

Millions have been inspired by the interspiritual thoughts and practice of Vietnamese Zen Buddhist monk Thich Nhat Hanh. Introduced to the West by Thomas Merton in the 1960s, he originally became known for his indigenous opposition to the Vietnam War. His whole life has been dedicated to the reconciliation of people at war with one another, an effort for which Dr. Martin Luther King Jr. nominated him for the Nobel Peace Prize. In more recent years, he has devoted considerable effort to bringing Christianity and Buddhism together, showing the common ground the traditions share. Although he is a devoted Buddhist and an accomplished spiritual teacher in his tradition, he is committed to a permanent friendship between these two venerable faiths.[8]

Thich Nhat Hanh embodies a gentleness and determination established on humility, simplicity, and compassion. His profound awareness is evident every time he walks into a room, sits on a chair, speaks to a group, or gives someone a drink of water. He is an icon of loving compassion, gentleness, and peace.

Rabbi Zalman Schachter-Shalomi

One of the most unusual and colorful spiritual masters of the last several decades, Rabbi Zalman Schachter-Shalomi is a great genius of interspiritual wisdom and a living master of the Jewish mystical tradition. The rabbi is an inspiring man whose heart is wide open to all the great streams of wisdom around the world.

I met him for the first time at the Future Visions Conference within the 2000 State of the World Forum in New York. I was impressed not only by his welcoming openness, but his easy comfort with advaita, sufism, satori, fana — experiences from all over the spiritual map. He was completely at home in all the traditions, though firmly rooted in his Jewishness.

As an interspiritual mystic, he has found the way to relate what is deepest in Judaism — its mystical insight — to what is deepest in every other tradition, that is, the mystical present in them. Reb Zalman is one of those rare spiritual teachers who puts everyone he meets at ease with his effortless charm and wisdom. His presence is as much an interspiritual teaching as his words.

Universal Mysticism

Interspirituality is essentially an agent of a universal mysticism and integral spirituality. We often walk the interspiritual or intermystical path in an intuitive attempt to reach a more complete truth. That final integration, a deep convergence, is an integral spirituality. Bringing together all the great systems of spiritual wisdom, practice, insight, reflection, experience, and science provides a truly integral understanding of spirituality in its practical application in our lives, regardless of our tradition. Interspirituality presupposes an integral vision, in terms of all the traditions. In the same way, integral spirituality must include all forms of spirituality. Integral spirituality in its own course becomes a universal mysticism.

All forms of spiritual life contribute to this universal mystical understanding, suggesting what is required to lead a *whole* spiritual life. Each spiritual tradition contributes insights, methodologies, psychological processes, and mystical experiences. Interspirituality requires all this spiritual wealth for our future work in transforming the human family.

All forms of spirituality also contribute methods to integrate body, mind, and spirit. At one time or another, most of us have asked, "How is the physical body related to the mind, and how can the mind and body serve the spirit, the ultimate openness to the Divine?" Such questions demand that we find the best means to bring about this kind of integration. Each tradition emphasizes different aspects of development, though some lack a clear understanding of how to reach complete integration. That is precisely why we need all forms of spiritual development, no matter how foreign they may seem to us initially. Integral spirituality is holistic; it represents a seamless garment in the human search for Ultimate Reality. Integral mysticism unites all forms of spirituality in itself in a perspective of ultimacy, when we step back far enough to see and experience a unifying vision of the totality of experience.

Universal mysticism means inclusivity of insight, experience, psychological penetration, approaches to the Source, the Divine, Infinite Consciousness. It seeks to reveal and celebrate what is truly universal in humankind's understanding of the Divine. It is imperative for us to walk into this future with confidence and wholeness. If our approach to the spiritual life is exclusivist or reductionist, we will only divide the human family, breed conflict, and isolate cultures in dangerous mental prisons of misunderstanding and distrust. It is critical that we seek an integral spiritual vision, a universal mysticism that gathers together spiritual treasures from among the cultures of the world, humankind's collective inner attainment throughout tens of millennia. This universal mysticism belongs to us all!

INTEGRAL SPIRITUALITY

Integral spirituality's horizon is vast, including many layers of insight, meaning, experience, and ideals. It includes the overarching, organizing principle of each spiritual tradition; all dimensions of awareness; the body, mind, and spirit; the conscious, unconscious, and superconscious; spirituality united with all other branches of knowledge; and the nine practical elements of mature spirituality outlined below.

Every spiritual tradition, like every religion, possesses a basic, primary insight that organizes its whole notion of the spiritual life. These overarching, organizing insights come under many names: God, Spirit, the Divine, the Source, the Tao, the One, the Unmoved Mover, the boundless consciousness, the perfected state of enlightenment, the Great Mystery. Integral spirituality takes in these organizing insights, each based on direct, unmediated experience. Each is valid in its own way, and each plays a role. Some converge or are similar, while others seem radically different. Yet each enriches our understanding of the whole. The first focus of integral spirituality would thus have to be an inclusive understanding of the nature of Ultimate Reality.

Its next focus might be on all the dimensions of awareness: the metaphysical, epistemological, mystical, and moral, which I will briefly consider in the next chapter. It would stress these dimensions in each form of spirituality, that is, how each conceives and experiences them. A culling of the immense wisdom of each tradition should result in a larger picture or understanding of these areas of knowledge within the spiritual life. The various approaches are then harmonized in this larger view.

Integral spirituality also relates to the human as a composite of body, soul, and spirit. It acknowledges that there are actually three principal parts to our nature and well-being, and that for our lives to be full, they must work together. The body is the material aspect of our life that interacts with the world, the

natural environment, and all other beings. The soul is vivifica-
tion — the force that brings life and which mediates between
body and spirit. The spirit is a transcendent openness to the
Divine, an existential capacity for relationship with it.

Integral spirituality also unifies the triad of conscious,
unconscious, and superconscious. The conscious life of the
person must unite with the unconscious, twilight domain of
the soul, and these two with the superconscious reality of the
Divine. Spiritual practice slowly breaks down the sense of separation among these three forms of consciousness, uniting
them so that they work together to refine us. Integral spirituality is connected with all branches of knowledge, because each
branch implies every other. In the ordinary growth of the inner
journey, integral spirituality draws on psychology, anthropology, physics, biology, and others, as each of these disciplines
contributes insight and direction. Mathematics, ecology, political science, and sociology also have important implications
for an integral spirituality. All branches of knowing are part of
the ultimate thrust of the overarching reality, which is essentially mystical. Great mathematicians, for instance, have
acknowledged the mystical divine mind present in upper levels
of mathematics. In medicine, researchers are discovering more
and more an integral understanding of how mind and spirit
are essential to the health of the body. In our spiritual lives,
every avenue of human knowledge can aid our development.

Finally, and probably most important for the individual,
integral spirituality includes nine practical elements drawn
from the great systems of the world's spiritual traditions: (1)
moral capacity, (2) solidarity with all sentient beings, (3) deep
nonviolence, (4) spiritual practice, (5) mature self-knowledge,
(6) humility, (7) simplicity of lifestyle, (8) selfless service and
compassionate action, and (9) prophetic voice and action.[9]

These are the nitty-gritty transformative elements of any serious form of the inner experience. If we were to bring together a representative from each tradition of spiritual wisdom, several accomplished teachers or realized masters, we would soon discover they all shared the same qualities. They would all exhibit a similar development of sensitivity, love, kindness, compassion, and mercy. They would all have progressed in these nine attitudes, virtues, and activities.

First, all would be disciplined in a substantial daily spiritual practice, from which the other qualities would result. Their moral capacity would be completely and organically actualized, directly springing from the depths of awareness. Each would have a deep understanding of the intrinsic interdependence of all beings and so would revere the preciousness and dignity of all life. They would all be committed to not harming. Each would possess an accurate self-knowledge grounded in humility of heart. They would be examples of simplicity in how they live and use this world's resources. Their love, sensitivity, and compassion would compel them to serve the needs of others. Finally, having the courage, integrity, and authenticity of their wisdom, they would each be prophetic voices in this world, working against the deception, propaganda, manipulation, exploitation, injustice, oppression, and inequality that exist everywhere.

More and more, the integral approach will become the norm in the pursuit of knowledge. Because of its ultimate importance in and urgency to our lives, an integral spirituality will no doubt continue to emerge. Only such an approach will ultimately satisfy our search for wholeness, giving us a mature understanding of our common nature and an expanded vision of how all the pieces of humankind's spiritual wisdom fit together in each of us.

THE CHRISTIAN-BUDDHIST DIALOGUE

It is sometimes difficult to imagine the genuine converging of ancient and disparate religious traditions. Many traditions have developed for so long with no acknowledged relation to the others that union seems impossible. Yet I believe just the opposite is true. Let us look, for example, at the relationship between two of the greatest, and seemingly most different, traditions. Just as the movement of interspirituality serves the revelation of a universal mysticism, so does the Buddhist-Christian relationship. Not only is there viable common ground between these two traditions, but together these two venerable ways have a responsibility higher than that of preserving themselves.

The most obvious area of commonality between Buddhism and Christianity is the focus on and experience of consciousness. Both traditions exist in and through awareness and self-awareness. They are not independent of consciousness, but intimately connected to it. Thought as self-awareness surrounds these two traditions, and both exist in a web of interdependence within consciousness in its more subtle forms. Both these paths share mystical consciousness and in fact seek that nexus of experience, insight, realization, and action. Although the ways they speak of their insights, methods, and goals are different, they are interacting with the same realm of being, of subtle, spiritual reality.

The two traditions also share another important focus: unitive awareness. Both aim at integrated consciousness, or nonduality. While all forms of mysticism are unitive, this focus is especially clear in Buddhist and Christian esotericism. The real knowledge of how all sentient beings are deeply interconnected unites these two wisdom systems further. They are both keenly aware of this underlying unity of creation, how all things share in a cosmic community of interdependence.

Christianity and Buddhism are also highly aware morally. Christians and Buddhists are keenly responsive to people's sufferings and have exquisitely evolved goals of love, charity, compassion, kindness, and mercy. The Buddhist understanding of compassion is probably the most advanced in the world, while the Christian practice of selfless love is equally unsurpassed.

There is, I believe, a real possibility of synthesis, or higher common ground, that can integrate the two in a new relationship. This synthesis brings together two fundamental realities. The first is the essential Buddhist insight of dependent arising, which states that all sentient beings are bound together in a cosmic web of interdependence — that they are intimately, intrinsically, and existentially connected to one another. While this metaphysical principle is a basic truth of Buddhism, on which the whole edifice of the dharma is erected, it can also be related to the ultimate principal insight and experience of the Christian faith, that of the Divine.

In Christianity, God, the Divine Reality, is the Source of all that is and binds all being, reality, and life together. This Ultimate Reality is related to the Buddhist reality of the intrinsic interconnectedness of all sentient beings. If I could sum up this shared belief, I would formulate it as "the Divine as the matrix of dependent arising." Though this concept sounds simple, this subtlety of perspective isn't easy to understand. The question is not, and can never be, which tradition holds the most accurate view of reality but how are both traditions true. And they are *both* ultimately true.

Just as the Divine encompasses all of reality, this reality and all the beings that compose or inhabit this reality are part of a universal cosmic order, a community of interconnection. This interdependence of all sentient beings within the overarching cosmic community exists within a medium of awareness, and that medium is the Divine itself. The Divine is the matrix, the container, the enveloping nature, the womblike place that holds all beings in interconnection. This Divine Reality is the very force of relationship among all sentient beings and reality itself. It is the mystical glue that holds everything together in itself. It is the connectivity in the interconnection, the dependence in the interdependence of all sentient beings.

Some may protest that I am imposing the Divine, through synthesis, on the Buddhists. Yet the Buddha himself, though silent about God, did convey something of the reality of the Divine in what I call his lotus teaching. When the Buddha was asked if God exists, he responded by smiling and simply holding up a lotus flower. I believe the Buddha's enigmatic response holds immense significance, but its meaning must be gleaned from the Hindu tradition, out of which the Buddha taught. When the Buddha responded to this important question, he was drawing on his knowledge of the great Chandogya Upanishad. This oldest of the 108 Upanishads was composed 1,200 years before the Buddha's birth, and in its oral tradition, may be a thousand years older:

> In the center of the castle of Brahman, our own body, there is a small shrine in the form of a lotus-flower, and within that can be found a small space. We should find who dwells there, and we should want to know him. And if anyone asks, "Who is he who dwells in a small shrine in the form of a lotus-flower in the center of the castle of Brahman? Whom should we want to find and to know?" We can answer: "The little space within the heart is as great as this vast universe. The heavens and the earth are there, and the sun, and the moon, and the stars; fire and lightning and winds are there; and all that now is and all that is not; for the whole universe is in Him and He dwells within our heart."[10]

This Upanishad, I suggest, was the very text the Buddha had in mind. The Buddha was communicating a simple truth: God does exist but is a matter of experience accessed through meditation. The Buddha was directing his listeners' attention not simply to this text, but more basically to the experience of looking within, to the lotus of the heart, where the Divine dwells.[11]

AN INTERSPIRITUAL MYSTIC
IN AN INTERSPIRITUAL WORLD

We are now firmly in the interspiritual age; we are ineluctably part of this historical process. It will become more deeply imbedded in culture, society, and the future of civilization. More and more I think of myself as an interspiritual mystic in an interspiritual world. This is the challenge in my life. I find it both fascinating and exciting, but also at times a bit confusing, since there is so much to process and integrate. Though I am committed to the interspiritual life, I am equally a Christian contemplative.

If the present is prologue, then the interspiritual movement in the course of the third millennium will take root everywhere, granting people endless options for their spiritual life. Although the world religions will remain an integral part of humanity's culture and identity, containing as they do vast repositories of wisdom and tradition, they will no longer divide peoples as before, because everyone will understand that what unites us is not religion, but spirituality, which can be said to be the real "religion" of humankind. Interspiritual communities will be common, and many people will be comfortable in more than one tradition. Every corner of the earth will see members of the various traditions working together in the creation and governance of a civilization of love. Then the human family will have come of age, and its members will realize their innate vocation to be community for one another, assisting in the growth of all.

A UNIVERSAL ORDER OF MYSTICS AND PRACTITIONERS

As the world moves toward an interspiritual future, new institutions will arise, and new movements will form to nurture community among members of the various traditions. Diversity in faith, practice, and spiritual life is a fundamental fact of life in the third millennium. History clearly shows that movements emerge to meet the needs of the people in every age. Our age clearly requires a way to promote and guide the precious and hard-won victory of the interfaith encounter.

What I propose is a loose network around the world welcoming members from all the world's religions, and those with no particular tradition at all. A universal, cross-cultural, and inclusive interspiritual order is a real possibility. Guarding the value of spiritual diversity is precious work in this contradictory age. This interspiritual order would be open to all genuine seekers of truth. It would include men, women, and children — married and single, young and old, educated and uneducated, clear and confused, and everything in between. It would welcome anyone with an open heart and mind. It is only when we learn to live together in concrete ways that the human community will evolve beyond the narrowness of our small groups and embrace a new identity.

CHAPTER 10

Living in the
Heart of Awareness

Every day, virtually everywhere, we can discover small and great acts of awareness. One day, my Uncle John was sitting on a park bench in Hartford's Bushnell Park, with the state capitol dome looming in the background. A woman was standing about ten feet away, speaking loudly and angrily to some unseen audience. After listening to her for a while, Uncle John gently, and with some humor, reached out to this troubled woman. "It can't be all that bad," he said. She turned to him, glaring. "How do you know, anyway?" she blurted. Uncle John laughed. "Well, I've been around a while, and I have some idea what you're going through," he said. "You do?" "Yes, I really do!" he replied. "Do you want to talk about it? Let's go get a nice cup of coffee." "I don't drink coffee," she pointed out. "I much prefer tea." "Then let's go," Uncle John offered, and off they went to a diner across from the railroad station.

Uncle John was alert to this poor soul's plight — he saw

that she was asking for help, for someone to listen to her. Uncle John possessed an aware mind and a generous heart. He was keenly discerning of human nature. Firmly rooted in the present, he was able to respond to her distress and anxiety. He was present to her need simply to have some kind person listen to her and perhaps encourage her in some way.

Encounters like this take place every day, all over the world; they are vitally important to the mystic. These connections are meant to happen, and when they do, they provide a possibility for the one who responds to grow as well as an opportunity for the one in need to receive kindness. In the following section, I will examine the fundamental nature of this precious form of consciousness and how it relates to the Divine. I will present a number of examples of genuine awareness at work in various lives, explore the elements of awareness, and conclude with a vision of an aware humanity.

THE NATURE OF AWARENESS

I distinguish between two forms of awareness — horizontal and vertical. Vertical awareness always relates to the transcendent Mystery, while the horizontal relates to our relationships to others, whether they be people, other sentient beings, the natural world, or even the entire cosmos. Most important, horizontal and vertical awareness become integrated in the contemplative process as it matures, when we encounter the Divine in everyone and everything. And both directions display themselves in four dimensions of knowing, each implicating and reflecting the others like a hologram.

These are the four elements present in awareness: metaphysical, epistemological, mystical, and moral dimensions — four ways of revealing, or "translating," the mystery of the Divine and applying it to our human condition. First, the metaphysical, as grounded in the transcendent One, is limitless vertical truth. The epistemological, or what we can know, is moment by moment a horizontal reality pointing to its vertical Source. The mystical, from the horizontal into the boundless, is the spacious verticality of the Divine. Finally, the moral combines transcendent vertical awareness with the horizontal — appropriate attitudes and actions in everyday life. In its spiritual expression, developing from its moral character, awareness is love in action, and the attributes of limitless sensitivity, kindness, compassion and mercy — actual acts of living.

Awareness in its vertical dimension gives us a direct understanding of the structure and content of reality, being, life — metaphysical knowledge. Or, I should say, it grants us understanding, through realization of that mystery that accounts for the content and structure in reality, life, and being. This quality of awareness emanates from consciousness, which is Spirit — a boundless, undetermined actuality. Metaphysical awareness allows us to know realities that are beyond the normal range of our senses; it brings us into contact with what is ultimately real, presenting to us the larger, indeed largest, view of the real. It is to see, even in fleeting glimpses, the grand scheme of things, how it is sustained, and to where it will return in a final culmination.

The epistemological dimension of awareness is the realization of what we can know of the nature and purpose of reality, being, and life. It is a knowledge of knowing itself, including the limits of knowing. This knowing, or direct, unmediated consciousness, puts us into contact with what is ultimately real. This knowing is certain of what is real and abidingly true. It is the conviction that comes from being in unmediated contact with Spirit. Direct contact with the Divine gives us the essential kind of knowing that grounds our life and purpose in the world. This epistemological aspect of awareness is grounded in pure intuitive knowing, which like metaphysical, mystical, spiritual, and moral knowledge is immediately given with little effort. It is a holistic gazing on the eternal Now in which all knowledge is available to us. When anything is experienced in this way, there is no room for doubt.

The mystical dimension of knowing, the direct awareness of Ultimate Reality, is more intimate than either the epistemological and metaphysical levels, which, although involving intuition, are rational modes of becoming aware of the real. It is relationship with the Divine through union with it, or it is ultimate realization of consciousness. Again, this consciousness is Spirit. In my experience, mystical awareness is knowing God directly through God's enveloping Presence and attaining, through God's awareness, an utterly, absolutely certain knowledge that is with me all the time. Mystical awareness is qualitatively different from all other forms of cognition; it is a new kind of knowing, an expanded range, not confined by the limitations of sensory and rational consciousness.

Mystical, or contemplative, awareness is one of the essential goals of a monk or mystic in the world. It presents us with the Real, and nothing is more certain than this knowledge — this intense, all-encompassing awareness. It is a very subtle form of knowing. It has an existential character that cannot be expressed in language, concepts, images, or any of the usual means we employ to explain what we know. It is a living, vivifying Presence. On a more mundane level, mystical awareness is, for me, primarily being conscious of God's Presence most of the time. When I am quiet enough to allow God's Presence to communicate itself to me, and both of us are silently present to each other, it is there. At times the Divine Presence will overpower me with love, consolation, or insight. The immediate effect within me, in the center of my own subjectivity, in the heights of interiority, is joy, an indescribable bliss that only God can give.

The moral dimension of awareness is recognizing true and infinite love, compassion, kindness, and sensitivity, as the Divine spontaneously expresses itself, in us, through our actions, our words, and our thoughts. When we are in total conformity and union with the Spirit, we become morally aware. At one level, moral awareness is simply knowing what is right, and that means knowing what reflects the character of love and compassion. But it is also something more: acting and being from the *real*, which is boundless, selfless love and compassion. The morally aware person, in the spiritual sense, acts in relationship to the Divine, is inspired by God's love, mercy, kindness, compassion, and sensitivity. For anyone who reaches this level of knowing, morality becomes their nature. They don't look to external norms of ethics in order to be good, because they have chosen love in the deepest center of their willing, knowing, and being. They have *become* compassion and love.

Love in Action

Such people do exist. For example, a dear friend of mine, Judy, has awakened to the all-encompassing practical awareness of the mystical life. Judy and I were initiated into Christian *sannyasa* by Father Bede Griffiths in India a day apart from each other. Judy is a nurse and for eighteen years had been a member of the Maryknoll congregation of missionary sisters. After meeting Bede Griffiths during his first visit to America in 1965, she became intensely interested in Indian spirituality and mysticism. Some years later, she left the Maryknoll sisters and went off to Bede's community, Shantivanam. Judy learned yoga, eventually becoming a talented teacher of this spiritual discipline and a master of meditation. She would meditate three or four hours a day, do an hour of yoga and a few hours of *lectio divina*, or spiritual reading, in her vertical quest for the Absolute.

For twenty-two years, Judy gave her life selflessly to the poorest of the poor in the villages of Bangladesh. She lived in the same manner as those she served, eating the same food, wearing a plain sari and shawl, and sleeping on a mat in a tiny room of a mud hut. She never charged for her endless services to these worthy people, nor was she sponsored by any organization. Rather, by working as a nurse in the United States for half a year, she could save the money necessary to sustain her for two or more years on the subcontinent. Judy's holiness is grounded in an abiding joy and a refreshing sense of humor. I'm always delighted to see her, and not just because she laughs at my silly jokes. This unknown heroine of mercy, who has saved the lives of countless children and adults, while comforting the sick and dying, is a model of the active mystic contemplative, working behind the scenes to transform the world by putting love into action. She has found the perfect balance of horizontal and vertical awareness. All holiness of life comes to the same fruition in every tradition: love in intention, thought, word, and deed. There is no substitute for this high moral quality. Responding to a homeless person, working with inner-city kids, visiting elderly shut-ins, spending time with the sick, and building homes for the poor are all examples of love in action. All these acts require a certain degree of generosity and awareness, particularly in the horizontal dimension.

Love in action, thought, and being is also a matter of sensitivity. We all know it takes real sensitivity to love selflessly. And sensitivity is itself a highly refined form of awareness, a gentle knowing of the preciousness of each person, each animal, each plant. Sensitivity is a vast understanding, intuitively grounded and cultivated in the school of spiritual practice. It is the nature of the mind, the empathic power to connect with others. When this inborn capacity is developed in the rough and tumble of life, it results in a natural tendency to be exquisitely aware and affirming of others. Sensitivity cannot be contained; it is boundless and free, giving to whomever it chooses.

Awareness, in its moral, existential expression, in the inner life of the person, and in the outer responses to others, is also kindness, a highly developed charity to everyone that radiates forth from the person like the warmth of the sun's rays. In each case of these attributes, one becomes them; they are not external to us. We are them, as the Divine is. Awareness is a process of becoming "deified" — God-like in our thoughts, desires, motivations, and especially our actions. Kindness, compassion, love, and mercy guide us on all these levels of our attention, mediating among our deepest commitment of the heart, the thrust toward holiness, and all those we meet in the course of our earthly life.

LIVING EXAMPLES OF AWARENESS

In the deserts of Egypt, Syria, and Palestine in the fourth century arose a very human and divine wisdom. The desert fathers and mothers cultivated an awareness I would call Christian humanism, which showed in how they treated one another. This humanism always revolved around charity toward one another, a listening with deep attention to the needs of others. At the same time, they were completely dedicated to fiery contemplative prayer. Two examples from Thomas Merton's *The Wisdom of the Desert* illustrate the dual human and divine qualities of this robust, earthy spirituality. These examples, like the previous example of Uncle John, demonstrate a clear horizontal awareness. Horizontal awareness is an attitude toward others governed by compassion, kindness, love, and a far-reaching sensitivity.

The first example points to the importance of nonjudgment, the perils of being a busybody, and the necessity of silence: "One of the elders said: A monk ought not to inquire how this one acts, or how that one lives. Questions like this take us away from prayer and draw us on to backbiting and chatter. There is nothing better than to keep silent."[1] This instance of human awareness shows humility, charity, and insight into prayer through silence. It is a human awareness shaped by the Divine, through contemplative prayer in the silence of the heart. This is the vertical dimension opening up to God, the Ultimate Reality.

The second example from the desert tradition emphasizes the fiery prayer of contemplation; it reveals the jewel of mystical wisdom in the hearts of these fourth-century souls of the desert: "Abbot Lot came to Abbot Joseph and said: 'Father, according as I am able, I keep my little rule, and my little fast, my prayer, meditation and contemplative silence; and according as I am able I strive to cleanse my heart of thoughts: now what more should I do?' The elder rose up in reply and stretched out his hands to heaven, and his fingers became like ten lamps of fire. He said: Why not be totally changed into fire?"[2]

This metaphor for mystical union, for being integrated with God in the intimacy of prayer — which becomes a communion of knowledge and love — is the vertical height of awareness in the Christian tradition, though many other traditions employ similar metaphors. It is the spacious awareness the Divine gives us of itself — as well as the very striving for this consciousness in contemplative or mystical practice.

Though not a desert father, St. Francis of Assisi was just as aware and had much in common with members of the earlier tradition. He had many experiences of deep awareness in his relatively short life of forty-three years. They ranged from ecstatic absorptions in the contemplation of God, to perceptions of the Divine Presence in nature and its creatures, to the understanding of God's subtle Presence in the disguised forms that most people miss. The saint of Assisi was a master of awareness, particularly its subtler forms.

Francis lived a privileged life as the son of a wealthy Assisi cloth merchant, Pietro Bernadone. Everything he wanted was given him, including the finest clothing. Francis dressed like a noble; in fact, his boyhood dream was to become one. One day Francis happened on a beggar in rags on a side street in Assisi. He embraced the beggar, then started to remove his cloak and tunic, offering to exchange garments with the beggar. The man was delighted, no doubt thinking to himself, "What a crazy sucker Francis is; he's got too much money for his own good." Francis perceived the Divine Presence in the beggar, saw his precious value, and had compassion for his destitute state. After trading their clothing, Francis again embraced him, smiled beatifically, and walked away, singing joyfully. The saint was beginning to realize that he had to be free of his attachments to wealth, clothing, food, and titles. He saw in this beggar an opportunity to become nonpossessive and to respond to the desperate plight of this poor soul before him. At the same time, he realized this encounter was an opportunity to deepen his relationship with God in his practice of love in action. This incident from the saint's life clearly shows the integration of the horizontal and vertical dimensions of the spiritual life.

A more contemporary spiritual figure relates how this kind of awareness is at the heart of the monk's vocation. I've known a fascinating Trappist monk by the name of Father Theophane Boyd for more than thirty years. Theophane, which means manifestation of God, was a member of Thomas Keating's St. Joseph's Abbey in Spencer, Massachusetts. Theophane is the author of the spiritual classic *Tales of the Magic Monastery*.[3] I talk with him every time I have the chance to visit his home, St. Benedict's Monastery, in Snowmass, Colorado.

Theo is a poet and spiritual teacher who reminds me of the wizard Gandalf in J.R.R. Tolkein's *Lord of the Rings* trilogy. In one of our early conversations, knowing how much I wanted to be a monk, he shared with me a very short but wise poem: "What is a monk? Beyond monk!" This piece of Christian near haiku sums up volumes of insight into the vocation of the monk. It addresses our tendency to attach ourselves to external forms and empty rituals. The essence of being a monk is a search, not the external form of looking like a monk. The search for God transcends the monastic state; it's what we should all be doing. It is also a journey of sharing life with your brother monks in the one common quest. Again, monastic life combines the vertical — the search for God — and the horizontal — harmony with our brothers and sisters.

An example of a more vertical kind of awareness comes directly from the life of Thomas Merton, near the end of his life. Years before his tragic death in 1968 (he was electrocuted by a fan in Bangkok, where he was attending a conference) Merton had been reading Eastern classical texts from the Hindu, Buddhist, and Taoist traditions, widening his awareness of Eastern spiritual insight. In his *Asian Journal*, Merton relates an explosion of awareness that occurred for him at the Buddhist shrine of Polonnaruwa. Two large statues rest there, an eighty-foot reclining Buddha with his eyes closed, representing him in death, and the standing figure of his beloved disciple Ananda. As he stood gazing at these magnificent images, a powerful reality burst into Merton's perception:

> Looking at the figures I was suddenly, almost forcibly, jerked clean out of the habitual, half-tied vision of things, and an inner clarity, as if exploding from the rocks themselves, became evident and obvious. The queer *evidence* of the reclining figure, the smile, the sad smile of Ananda standing with arms folded (much more "imperative" than Da Vinci's *Mona Lisa* because completely simple and straightforward). The thing about all this is that there is no puzzle, no problem, and really no "mystery." All problems are resolved and everything is clear. The rock, all matter, all life, is charged with *dharmakaya* (the body of reality)...everything is emptiness and everything is compassion. I don't know when in my life I have ever had such a sense of beauty and spiritual validity running together in one aesthetic illumination. Surely, with Mahabalipuram (Hindu shrine, series of ancient temples south of Madras) and Polonnaruwa my Asian pilgrimage has come clear and purified itself. I mean, I know and have seen what I was obscurely looking for.[4]

This is a classic dawning of a mystical, metaphysical insight communicated through art. I call this a vertical direction of awareness, because its form and content concern ultimate realities.

A more horizontal example of simple yet deep awareness comes from my former community of Hundred Acres Monastery. I witnessed this particular example at least fifty times during the life of its founder, Father Paul Fitzgerald, who died in 1991. Spike, a black-and-white Angora cat, was one of the many animals at Hundred Acres. He had been in a terrible fight and suffered from ugly gashes and wounds when he was brought to Hundred Acres by a member of the community.

This wonderful feline ended up staying for years. He slept in his favorite seat in the barn, where we all lived. This seat was near the bay window looking out on a bird feeder, and Father Paul liked that seat as well. He would say his office or prayers there every morning. But, of course, many mornings Spike was curled up in the chair. Father Paul would never disturb him but would quietly take another nearby chair. In contrast, another member of the community would unceremoniously drop Spike on the floor if he wanted the seat. It was a small gesture, yet it revealed a great awareness of and sensitivity to the needs of others, whether animal or human.

To provide a more personal example, one summer, many years ago, when I was home from college in Hartford, Connecticut, I was repeating one of my favorite walks, downtown from my home. Just as I was coming to an unavoidable railway underpass, a man approached me on the street. He started talking to me in a friendly way, yet all of a sudden I knew he was a mugger. I remained calm and intuitively engaged him in conversation. I tried to look into his heart and see his deeper goodness and appeal to it as we walked through the tunnel together. It worked; he was distracted and only realized what had happened when we came out the other side. I simply decided I wasn't going to be a victim, that I'd reach out to him on a deeper level and change the structure of the encounter. The fellow was smiling as he walked away.

THE ELEMENTS OF AWARENESS

The elements of awareness encompass conscious knowing, the ability to read hearts, to be a healing, loving, compassionate presence, situated in the Now. They also encompass practical wisdom in every situation, the ability to enlarge perspective, to affirm others and promote dialogue and mutual understanding.

Conscious Knowing

Awareness, as an enhanced consciousness and heightened sensitivity to others, allows us to take in more of reality than many can manage. But while awareness can be overwhelming, in most cases, a person with subtle awareness becomes a healing, loving, compassionate being. He or she is always looking for ways to respond to others and to assuage suffering. A person walking with awareness exudes a confidence that inspires and attracts others who see. A presence flows through the aware person, a grace and humility, a holiness and love. People who are truly aware communicate the depth of their inner consciousness, their nearness to God, or the Spirit, through their presence and their actions.

Most important, this awareness is always situated in the Now, in the integrity of the present moment with all its opportunities and challenges. I once heard the Trappist writer and abbot Basil Pennington talk about the life of the hermit. Near the end of his talk, he suddenly blurted out, "God is Now. Everything else is sin!" He was probably just trying to get our attention, but he said something very significant: that everything important is happening Now. God is Now. The Divine will embraces Now; to dwell on the past or the future misses the point. We must cultivate our awareness of Now, and the consciousness of this Now is the intersection, ultimately, of the vertical and horizontal.

In his classic work *The Power of Now*, the writer and teacher Eckhart Tolle emphasizes in great detail the utter reality of the Now. He has clearly seen that to understand the Now is the key to spiritual realization and enlightenment:

> Have you ever experienced, done, thought, or felt anything outside the Now? Do you think you ever will? Is it possible for anything to happen or *be* outside the Now? The answer is

obvious, is it not? Nothing ever happened in the past; it happened in the Now. Nothing will ever happen in the future; it will happen in the Now. What you think of as the past is a memory trace, stored in the mind, of a former Now. When you remember the past, you reactivate a memory trace — and you do so now. The future is an imagined Now, a projection of the mind. When the future comes, it comes as the Now. When you think of the future, you do it now. Past and future obviously have no reality of their own. Just as the moon has no light of its own, but can only reflect the light of the sun, so are past and future only pale reflections of the light, power, and reality of the eternal present. Their reality is "borrowed" from the Now.[5]

Just as all reality is mediated through consciousness, all time exists in the Now. This Now, however, exists only in consciousness, in the vast, eternal awareness of the Divine itself.

Wisdom

Another element of awareness is wisdom. In its horizontal dimension, wisdom means the knowledge of what is good, necessary, and appropriate. It is, first and foremost, knowing the truth of every situation one encounters, as we saw illustrated in the previous example of Uncle John. Solomon applied his celebrated wisdom to the difficult case of the two women who claimed the same infant; the king had to decide who was telling the truth.[6] He ordered the baby to be cut in half, knowing that the real mother would rather give up the child than allow it to be harmed in any way.

When Jesus encountered the woman accused of adultery, the scribes and Pharisees wanted to trap him. Mosaic law required that a woman caught in the act of adultery be stoned to death, and they wanted *him* to stone her. Jesus intuitively knew the wise course, what was truly just and compassionate. "'Let the one among you who is guiltless be the first to throw a stone at her,' he said. When they heard this they went away one by one."7 Both Christ and Solomon possessed the necessary perspective and wisdom for understanding the situations in which they found themselves. Solomon possessed a deep knowledge of human nature. Christ juxtaposed Mosaic law with the crowd's private sins. He knew they were all guilty and so was able to stir the shame of the tricksters.

In a similar way, Buddhists like Thich Nhat Hanh call for a larger perspective when they suggest that we search for someone's motivation in a confrontational situation. When we enlarge our perspective to include understanding of the real motivations behind hateful or annoying acts, we realize that deep down we hold compassion even for those we think we despise. The spiritually aware person is profoundly attuned to the presence of the Divine in each encounter with others.

Wisely aware people, such as those in the interfaith movement, build bridges between communities. They promote dialogue, friendship, and mutual understanding. They understand that these activities break down the walls that have separated us for millennia. Always looking for common ground, the wise seek opportunities for conversation across the boundaries of difference. Although they remain conscious of differences among the religions and cultures of the world, they look for places of collaboration, building habits of cooperation. Awareness, in this context, is the realization that what unites us is more important, and in fact more substantial, than what divides us. Preserving relationships among religions, nations, cultures, communities, and families always serves the higher good.

Ongoing dialogue is vital in this process of preserving relationships. In the exchange of knowledge, relationships increase

ɔssibility of awareness in the participants. As the Dalai
Lа..ı has so often remarked, "True dialogue is possible only
between friends," for friends are naturally open to one another.
This is why we must, through cultivating awareness, find common ground.

DIVINE AWARENESS

The Divine is pure sensitivity, infinite consciousness, cosmic
awareness, and an unlimited heart that is wise beyond comprehension.[8] The Divine also possesses infinite intelligence — not
the cold, analytical type but essential warmheartedness. God is
total heart. Love is the Spirit's only motivation. Nothing can
exceed love in priority, the most comprehensive reality. We have
little understanding of this kind of love; our experience of
human love is so limited, both in time and experience, compared to Divine Love, which knows no such limits; it is boundless, creative, wise, holy, and humorous. It is always responding,
always giving to us according to our nature and capacity.

God is also unlimited Light in every direction, an insight
found in most of the spiritual traditions. Tibetan esotericism
speaks of it as the Clear Light of the Void, which we encounter
at the end of our lives. Christian tradition says, "God is Light in
whom there is no darkness."[9] This is not simply a metaphor.
The scientist Peter Russell, in his book *From Science to God,*
sees a direct connection between light and consciousness,
identifying them with God. The Divine *is* literally light.[10]

The Divine is also boundless stillness, the stillness we can
touch in meditation, when we slow down and allow quiet to
invade our awareness. "Stillness is the greatest revelation,"
as a powerful Taoist aphorism goes. When we experience stillness, in any situation, we are also encountering the Divine.
Stillness is the stability and immutability of the Divine. What

truly is in itself has no need to change or to become. Stillness is the Presence flowing from itself and into itself, the reality of a self-subsisting identity that is complete, perfect, and passionately wanting to share itself with all other beings. All reality is within the infinite Divine, which is of the nature of openness and expansion. We have only to be still, quiet, and listen, and we will hear the Divine's symphony.

Toward an Aware Humanity

The above attributes would take root universally in an aware humanity. Such awareness would deepen and mature, sparking the social, political, and economic transformation of the human family. Enlightenment is the fullness of this awareness. This awareness on the moral level, in the existential requirement of each moment, is pure sensitivity. This depth of sensitivity embraces all; it regards everyone and everything, including other sentient beings, as having a precious value and dignity.

The center of awareness, of this sensitivity, this holy and active empathy, is consciousness — what Ken Wilber aptly calls "the eye of Spirit":

> When I rest in simple, clear, ever-present awareness, I am resting in intrinsic Spirit; I am in fact nothing other than witnessing Spirit itself. I do not become Spirit; I simply recognize the Spirit that I always already am. When I rest in simple, clear, ever-present awareness, I am the Witness of the World. I am the eye of Spirit. I see the world as God sees it. I see the world as the Goddess sees it. I see the world as Spirit sees it: every object an object of Beauty, every thing and event a gesture of the Great Perfection, every process a ripple in the pond of my own eternal Being, so much so that I do not stand apart as a separate witness, but find the witness is

one taste with all that arises within it. The entire Kosmos arises in the eye of Spirit, in the I of Spirit, in my own intrinsic awareness, this simple ever-present state, and I am simply that.[11]

Wilber has experienced that awareness that floods from his inner depths. He has discovered the Divine in the silence. It is to this profoundly urgent awareness that each one of us is called and destined. It is to this awareness that all monks or mystics are dedicated. There really is no other place to go and no other place to be. Ultimately, there is no escape from the eye of Spirit and the great joy, burden, and vision of the real inviting us to itself.

Toward a New
Catholicity

As a monk in the world, I've learned that a viable and authentic spiritual life is not only possible but essential for our common future — and so, hopefully inevitable, in one way or another, for all of us. Each one of us is a mystic; a monk dwells in each of our depths, just below our everyday awareness. For me, the mystical path means awakening this monk within and nurturing its development in encountering the world. This path is reinforced by spiritual practice, with its breakthroughs and graces; supported by like-minded friends, with their love and challenges; empowered by thoughtful navigations through the limitations of time, work, and money. It means living with compassion and love in the concreteness of daily encounters, especially with the most vulnerable. It means taking risks for the sake of justice, which requires us to speak the truth boldly, clearly, and firmly to power in all its forms, especially the political, economic, and religious.

Living the mystical life in our modern world means changing the self-understanding of our institutions, especially our spiritual ones. My challenge to the Church, the Catholic Church I belong to and which is my home, I believe, is an important part of my witness as a contemplative. It is with profound love that I call for the Church to engage the other religions and indeed all the critical issues humankind equally shares: the struggle for justice, the work for planetary peace, the promotion of ecological responsibility, the pursuit of interspirituality, and the work of building an economic, political, and social order with a heart — indeed, globalization with a heart. It will require the Church to open its arms to everyone: Jews, Hindus, Buddhists, Muslims, Sikhs, Jains, other Christians, all members of indigenous traditions, as well as humanists, agnostics, and atheists. This wider, indeed *catholic,* identity is the Church as the matrix. I believe it is necessary for the Church and a way forward into a renaissance of Catholicism.

The very core of this matrix is interspirituality, animated by the incandescence of awareness. This awareness is the inner, contemplative experience extending our insight in all situations. The Church as matrix would encompass the wisdom garnered through interspiritual exploration — the openness to and assimilation of spiritual treasures from all the traditions, along with scientific wisdom — thus enlarging the horizon of the human family's understanding far beyond petty tribalism.

Living the spiritual life isn't easy, whether in the cloister or in the world. We need all the help we can get, especially as we resist our hard secular culture. Being an engaged mystic in the world requires us to set aside all tribalism: ethnic, religious, intellectual, and cultural. It means seeking the universal present in all of us, while awakening others to it. No culture, religion, philosophy, or scientific enterprise has all the answers.

We need all these manifestations of the human search for the Ultimate.

A mystic must seek dialogue with his or her brothers and sisters in other faith traditions. These conversations always reveal common ground. And the mystical process creates an inner spaciousness of being that makes room for this common ground, that welcomes all diversity and otherness. This openness is progressive, ever extending itself to include more and more of *what is* — members of other traditions, genders, ages, orientations, species — reaching from the known into the great unknown, making inner space for what is beyond our own notions of reality. In all of this the Divine is both masking and revealing itself in a cosmic dance of otherness.

If we can learn to embrace this otherness, to heal the ancient divisions and misunderstandings of the past, if we can grant and accept forgiveness — always choosing the path of nonharming in relation to all of humankind, other natural beings, and the world around us — then we will have come of age as a species. Our spirituality will have prepared us for the next steps in our evolution, steps that will inevitably lead us into a larger identity and responsibility in the Divine Mystery. Each one of us has to stretch beyond self-interest — the confining concerns of our family, friends, community, religion, culture, nation, or even species. We must think in terms of the whole community of life.

I have witnessed growing sensitivity, compassion, love, mercy, and kindness in those who have accepted the invitation to walk the spiritual path. The spiritual journey, whether in the world or the cloister, is an infallible means to transform us into aware human beings. The truly aware radiate love and forgiveness. Their presence heals and transforms; it disarms hostility, confusion, ambiguity, and indifference. Confronting evil, injustice, violence, and tragedy, the awake maintain the essential perspective of wisdom, the awareness of the larger picture: the absoluteness of love. They call others, through their witness and presence, to consider this larger reality, which is often obscured in the heat of violence, confrontation, and war.

If, in the face of destruction, we are consistently loving, compassionate, and wise — while doing what must be done to protect the innocent — we will eventually help ourselves and our antagonists to realize something beyond hatred and violence. In a brief poem, Allen Ginsberg characterized the incisive quality of awakeness: "Holy is the supernatural extra brilliant intelligent kindness of the soul." Kindness is the essence of spiritual realization, the fruit of awareness. We can always remember as inspiration that the Dalai Lama's religion *is* kindness — both as practice and as fruit.

Finally, a vision of the future has emerged for me in the course of my spiritual journey. Again and again, it has appeared to me as I am returning from meditation: the necessity for a universal order of mystics or contemplatives. They would include people from all traditions and no tradition at all. They would be young and old, men and women, certain and skeptical, confused and enlightened. The movement's goal would be to provide a universal forum of diversity, bringing about openness to change by becoming agents of spiritual and intellectual ferment. Simply by being spiritual in a more spacious way — in an interspiritual way — it would broaden the horizon of our experience and knowledge. Its goal would be to enlarge our wisdom and our scope of action, to constantly radiate attitudes of charity, kindness, love, and compassion. The more this spirit spreads, the more it will awaken human consciousness to something greater than what we've known.

Let me conclude with a prayer: "O Blessed One, transform

us all into the boundless Love you are, and let us always radiate this Love to you, to one another, and to all those we meet — all sentient beings — unto eternal life." This prayer is both an intention and a practice, a practice that incarnates the intention in the center of our awareness. May this practice, this intention, this seed of realization, take root in us all and lead us into greater freedom, generosity, and change, culminating in a new human order: a civilization with a heart!

CHAPTER NOTES

INTRODUCTION

1 Raimundo Panikkar, ed. and trans., *The Vedic Experience: An Anthology of the Vedas for Modern Man and Contemporary Celebration.* (Pondicherry, India: All India Books, 1977), 436.

2 Thomas Keating, *Open Mind, Open Heart: The Contemplative Dimension of the Gospel* (Amity, N.Y.: Amity House, 1986), 29.

3 David Steindl-Rast, "Monastic Parenthood," in *Abba: Guides to Wholeness and Holiness East and West,* ed. James Sommerfeldt (Kalamazoo, Mich.: Cisterican Publications, 1982), 369.

4 Raimon Panikkar, *Blessed Simplicity: The Monk as Universal Archetype* (New York: Seabury Press, 1982), 10.

5 Panikkar, *Blessed Simplicity,* 16.

6 Matthew 25:34–40.

CHAPTER 1

1 Hebrews 13:14.

2 Mark Epstein, *Thoughts without a Thinker: Psychotherapy from a Buddhist Perspective* (New York: Basic Books, 1995), 45.

3   Bede Griffiths, *A Human Search: The Life of Bede Griffiths*, More than Illusion Films, 1993.

4   I have discussed this dimension of nature at great length in my book *The Mystic Heart: Discovering a Universal Spirituality in the World's Religions* (Novato, Calif.: New World Library, 1999), chapter 8.

5   Louis Bouyer et al., eds., *The Spirituality of the New Testament and the Fathers*, 3 vols. (New York: Seabury-Crossroad, 1968), 314.

6   Bouyer, *Spirituality of the New Testament*, 315.

CHAPTER 2

1   For Centering Prayer and its background, see Thomas Keating's *Open Mind, Open Heart: The Contemplative Dimension of the Gospel* (Rockport, Mass.: Element Books, 1986). See also Wayne Teasdale, *The Mystic Heart* (Novato, Calif.: New World Library, 1999) 132–34.

2   On spiritual practice, see Teasdale, *The Mystic Heart*, 128–41.

3   For more about *lectio divina*, see Teasdale, *The Mystic Heart*, 129–31.

4   "The Cloud of Unknowing" in *Classics of Western Spirituality*, James Walsh, ed. (New York: Paulist Press, 1981), 126.

5   See Teasdale, *Mystic Heart*, chapter 8.

6   Psalm 46:11.

7   Rig Veda X, 129. See Raimundo Panikkar, ed., *The Vedic Experience, Mantramanjari: An Anthology of the Vedas for Modern Man and Contemporary Celebration* (Pondicherry, India: All India Books, 1977), 58.

8   Genesis 1:2.

9   Genesis 2:7.

10 John 20:22.

11 Kieran Kavanaugh and Otilio Rodriguez, eds. and trans., *Collected Works of St. John of the Cross*, (Washington, D.C.: ICS Publications, 1973), 649.

12 See Teasdale, *Mystic Heart*, chaps. 5, 6, and 7.

CHAPTER 3

1   Campbell Bonner, ed., *A Papyrus Codex of the Shepherd of Hermas (Similitudes 2-9) with a Fragment of the Mandates,* (Ann Arbor: University of Michigan Press, 1934). See also Lage Pernveden, *The Concept of the Church in the Shepherd of Hermas* (Lund, Sweden: CWK Gleeup, 1966), and especially Carolyn Osiek, *Shepherd of Hermas: A Commentary* (Minneapolis, Minn.: Fortress Press, 1999), 41-59.

    A word about depicting the Church as feminine: The title, content, and purpose of this chapter, my own personal history, and the culture to which I and 1.2 billion others belong require me to refer to the Church as feminine. The word *church,* or *ecclesia,* is feminine, and it is feminine in all the European languages — only in English is it neuter. I believe the context of this chapter removes it from the charge of being sexist, or even antiquated. Here it is a question of cultural sensitivity, which is a two-way street. Latin is the official language of the Catholic Church, and the femininity of the Church is essential to her self-understanding.

2   Bonner, *Papyrus Codex,* 58.

3   Matthew 22:21, Mark 12:17, and Luke 20:25.

4   See chapters 1 and 2 of my last book, *The Mystic Heart* (Novato, Calif.: New World Library, 1999).

CHAPTER 4

1   Cicero, *L'amitie: Laelius de Amicitia,* Robert Combes, trans. (Paris: Bude, 1975).

2   Edith Hamilton and Huntington Cairns, eds., *The Collected Dialogues of Plato* (New York: Bollinggen, 1963), see *The Lysis.*

3   *The Basic Works of Aristotle,* Rich and Mckeon, ed. (New York, Random House, 1941), see Nichomachean Ethics, Bks. 8, 9, 10.6-8, on contemplation.

4   1 John 4:19.

A MONK IN THE WORLD

5   John 15:15.
6   Matthew 25:31–40.
7   Matthew 5:46.
8   John 13:23.
9   John 15:12–13.
10 For an excellent work on friendship in monasticism throughout history, see Brian McGuire's *Friendship and Community: The Monastic Experience, 350–1250* (Kalamazoo, Mich.: Cistercian Publications, 1988). See also Jean Leclercq's *The Love of Learning and the Desire for God: A Study of Monastic Culture* (New York: Fordham University Press, 1977).
11 Aelred of Rievaulx's writing is especially illustrative of the depth of commitment to spiritual friendship. See his *Spiritual Friendship*, Mary Eugenia Laker, trans. (Kalamazoo, Mich.: Cistercian Publications, 1974).
12 Cicero, *L'amitie*, 6, 2.
13 Gregory, *XL Homiliarum in Evangelia II, Homil.* 27.4 = PL 176:1207, and Isidore, *Etymologiarum sive Originum Libre XX*, W. M. Lindsay, ed. (Oxford: Clarndon Press, 1911), bk. x.
14 McGuire, *Friendship and Community*, 296.
15 Aelred of Rievaulx, *Spiritual Friendship*, 112.
16 McGuire, *Friendship and Community*, 244.
17 His Holiness the Dalai Lama, *Ethics for the New Millennium* (New York: Riverhead Books, 1999), 151.

CHAPTER 5

1   Immanual Kant, *The Critique of Pure Reason*, Norman Kemp Smith, trans. (New York: St. Martin's Press, 1965), 74–82.
2   *Baraka: A World beyond Words*, directed by Ron Fricke, 1992.
3   For a fine reflection on the nature of work, see Michael and Justine Toms, *True Work: Doing What You Love and Loving What You Do* (New York: Bell Tower, 1998).

CHAPTER 6

1   In the film *The Saint of Fort Washington* (Warner Home Video, 1993), Danny Glover and Matt Dillon play two homeless men trying to save enough money to get an apartment and find their way back into the regular world. The film shatters the stereotypes many have of the homeless.

2   Wayne Teasdale, *The Mystic Heart* (Novato, Calif: New World Library, 1999), 153.

3   For her autobiography, see *The Long Loneliness* (San Francisco: HarperCollins, 1997). Also see Robert Coles, *Dorothy Day: A Radical Devotion* (Reddington, Mass.: Addison-Wesley, 1987).

CHAPTER 7

1   *The Collected Dialogues of Plato,* ed. Edith Hamilton and Huntington Cairns (New York: Bollingen-Pantheon, 1966).

2   *Collected Dialogues,* vol. 7, 747–52.

3   *Collected Dialogues,* vol. 7, 747–48.

4   *Collected Dialogues,* vol. 7, 752.

5   See *A SourceBook for Earth's Community of Religions,* ed. Joel Beversluis (Grand Rapids, Mich.: CoNexus Press and Global Education Associates, 1995), 171.

6   *SourceBook,* 216–17.

CHAPTER 8

1   George Bosworth Burch, trans., *Bernard, Abbot of Clairvaux: The Steps of Humility* (Notre Dame, Ind.: University of Notre Dame Press, 1963).

2   Adalbert de Vogue, *The Rule of Saint Benedict: A Doctrinal and Spiritual Commentary* (Kalamazoo, Mich.: Cistercian Publications, 1983), 117–26.

3   Acts 17:28. Attributed to the Greek poet Epimenides.

CHAPTER 9

1 Foundation for Inner Peace, *A Course in Miracles* (New York: Viking, 1996).

2 For information, please contact the guest mistress at Osage Monastery, 18701 W. Monastery Road, Sand Springs, OK. 74063. Tel. (918) 245-2734.

3 Please write, call, or e-mail: "Friends of God" Dominican Ashram, 720 35th Street, Kenosha, WI 53140, (262) 658-1062, ashram@dominicans.org.

4 For details of his considerable mystical experience, see Abhishiktananda, *The Further Shore* (Delhi: ISPCK, 1975), and his masterpiece, *Saccidananda: A Christian Approach to Advaitic Experience* (Delhi: ISPCK, 1984).

5 I would suggest two of his books to get a deeper impression of his thought, experience, and insight. These would be: *Return to the Center* (Springfield, Ill.: Templegate, 1987), and his *A New Vision of Reality: Western Science, Eastern Mysticism and Christian Faith* (Springfield, Ill.: Templegate, 1989). See also my doctoral dissertation on Bede's thought, mysticism, and approach to Hinduism, called *Toward a Christian Vedanta: The Encounter of Hinduism and Christianity According to Bede Griffiths* (Bangalore, India: Asian Trading, 1987).

6 For a good book on her life, see Judith Cornell, *Amma: Portrait of a Living Sage* (San Francisco: William Morrow, 2001).

7 Panikkar has written nearly fifty books, but two that are representative of his thought include *The Vedic Experience* (Pondicherry, India: All India Books, 1983), and *Invisible Harmony: Essays on Contemplation and Responsibility* (Minneapolis, Minn.: Fortress Press, 1995).

8 See his books *Living Buddha, Living Christ* (New York: Riverhead, 1995), and *Going Home: Jesus and Buddha as Brothers* (New York: Riverhead Books, 1999).

9 I have developed these at considerable length in *The Mystic Heart* (Novato, Calif.: New World Library, 1999), chapters 5, 6, and 7.

10 Juan Mascaro, trans., *The Upanishads* (Baltimore, Md.: Penguin Books, 1965), Chandogya 8.1.

11 There are other indications of a theistic dimension to the Buddha's experience. See Jamshed Fozdar's *The God of Buddha* (Ariccia, Italy: Casa Editrice Baha'i Sri, 1995). For an exploration of theism in Tibetan Buddhism, see Alan Wallace's "Is Buddhism Really Nontheistic?" *Snow Lion,* vol. 15, no. 1, Winter 2000.

CHAPTER 10

1 Thomas Merton, *The Wisdom of the Desert: Sayings from the Desert Fathers of the Fourth Century* (New York: New Directions, 1972), 74.

2 Merton, *Wisdom of the Desert,* 50.

3 Theophane the Monk, *Tales of the Magic Monastery* (New York: Crossroad, 1984).

4 Patrick Hart et al., eds., *The Asian Journal of Thomas Merton,* (New York: New Directions, 1975), 233, 235–36.

5 Eckhart Tolle, *The Power of Now: A Guide to Spiritual Enlightenment* (Novato, Calif.: New World Library, 1999), 41–42.

6 3 Kings 3:27.

7 John 8:7–9.

8 I have written of the divine nature in *The Mystic Heart* (Novato, Calif.: New World Library, 1999), 76–77, 199–200, 224–26.

9 1 John 1:5.

10 Peter Russell, *From Science to God: The Mystery of Consciousness and the Meaning of Light* (Sausalito, Calif.: Peter Russell, 2000), see chapters 3, 5, 6, and 7. To order, www.peterrussell.org.

11 Ken Wilber, *The Eye of Spirit: An Integral Vision for a World Gone Slightly Mad* (Boston: Shambhala, 1997), 296.

INDEX

A

Abhishiktananda, 180, 182–83
Adam's Peak, 4–6
Aelred, 81–82
agape, xxxi, 78, 79, 126, 141
aikido, 94
Ammachi ("Amma"), 184
Ananda, 71
attachment, freedom from, 106
attention/attentiveness, 31;
    contemplative, 21
autonomy, 162
aware humanity, toward an, 213–14
awareness, 140; dimensions of,
    189, 192–93; elements of,
    198–99, 208–12; horizontal *vs.*
    vertical, 198–99, 207; and jus-
    tice, 140–43; living examples
    of, 203–8; nature of, 198–203

B

Baraka (film), 97
being, silence of, 33
Benedict, St., 161–62
Bernadone, Pietro, 204
Bernard, 81–82
Bonaventure, St., 7
boundary meltdown (religions),
    174
Boyd, Theophane, 206
Brief History of Everything, A
    (Wilber), xvii
Buddha, 71; on the Divine,
    194–95; on suffering,
    168–69
Buddhism, 106–7; Tibetan,
    145 (*see also* Dalai Lama).
    See also Christian-Buddhist
    dialogue

ABOUT THE AUTHOR

Brother Wayne Teasdale is a lay monk who combines the traditions of Christianity and Hinduism in the way of Christian sannyasa. An activist and teacher in building common ground between religions, Teasdale serves on the board of trustees of the Parliament of the World's Religions. As a member of the Monastic Interreligious Dialogue, he helped draft their Universal Declaration on Nonviolence. He is an adjunct professor at DePaul University, Columbia College, and the Catholic Theological Union, and coordinator of the Bede Griffiths International Trust. He is the author of *The Mystic Heart: Discovering a Universal Spirituality in the World's Religions*. He holds an M.A. in philosophy from St. Joseph College and a Ph.D. in theology from Fordham University. He lives at the Catholic Theological Union in Chicago and speaks throughout the world.